The

PocketScroll® Series

The Power of

A PocketScroll® Book

Teshuvah

An effective day by day guide

Rabbi Heshy Kleinman

best-selling author of *Praying with Fire*

Published and distributed by **MESORAH PUBLICATIONS, LTD.**
4401 Second Avenue / Brooklyn, N.Y. 11232 / (718) 921-9000

ISBN 10: 1-4226-1109-4
ISBN 13: 978-1-4226-1109-8

Printed in the United States of America

שמואל קמנצקי
Rabbi S. Kamenetsky

2018 Upland Way
Philadelphia, PA 19131

Home: 215-473-2798
Study: 215-473-1212

בס"ד יום א' ואתחנן לסדר

לכ' הרב הגאון ר' בער העניך קלויזנר שליט"א

המעלה רב בכולו דהכל[...]

הנ"ל לתמוך ידו ואותה בקלוש ושותפת את
הרבים דכולו הק' ואצ[...] אגלו[...] ר"ל דאמרו
האמרים שבחים נ[...] לבני ישראל דירד[...] הלכ[...]
לנדחתן שלא היתה להחמיר לבחמרי להבח[...] ומלה[...]
ולמ[...] קלוש ודפי, ש[...] הדרוך אל מאות הכבודים
דאות הל[...] שב[...] ח[...]נ[...] לחת מ[...] הרגי במאמרים

הידידו מברכו,

[חתימה] קמין ל[...]

(718) 436-1133

RABBI YAAKOV PERLOW
1569 - 47TH STREET
BROOKLYN N.Y. 11219

יעקב פרלוב
קהל עדת יעקב נאוואמינסק
ישיבת נאוואמינסק - קול יהודא
ברוקלין, נ.י.

בס"ד יום ג' אלול ה' תש"נ מברכין

הג"מ (?) הרב הגון ונעלה עולה וחרה בק' ק' [...] על כל אחדותי
"מתנחמת התעודה" גסקב התקדימא ו [...] מעלתו [...] לאור, והנני גלא
לרבותינו דקדמית הטיטו וכדברי חיבוק הרעיון הטוב לחזקים ח[...] והקדף
[...] ואם גם הירב בגאון לרבני חידוש [...] ואת הן ישם [...] קולו להגשר
[...] ולבה התעלות על [...] הגדל. [...] ברך הם [...] הגלת הגשר[...]
לכבוד לעולם. הנביזו [...]

הנה כעיקן ו[...]

יעקב ([...]) פרלוב

מכתב הסכמה מהרב הגאון ר' מתתיהו סולומן, שליט"א
משגיח דישיבת לאקווד

בס"ד

עש"ק פ' מסעי תשע"א לפ"ק
פה לייקווד יצ"ו

מאד נפלאתי על פעולות הגדולות אשר זכה ידידי כמוה"ר אברהם צבי
קליינמאן שליט"א להו"ל ספרי הדרכה בענין חיזוק לכמה מצות חשובות
אשר ערך בטוב טעם ודעת למשוך את לבם של אהב"י לקיימם מצות
באש והתלהבות ובעזה"י הי' לו הצלחה מרובה למעלה ראש להיות מזכה
את הרבים.
כעת נשאו לבו להעיר ולעורר על יסוד התשובה אשר כל בית ישראל
נשען עליה כי קרוב אליך הדבר מאד בפיך ובלבבך לעשותו.
הנני מברכו כאשר זכה עד עתה לזכות את הרבים בסייעתא דשמיא כן
יזכה עוד שרבים ישאבו ממעינותיו הטהורים גם מספר זה העוסקת
בהירות דרכי התשובה כי כל מימיו שאובים מבאר מים חיים של תוה"ק
להשקות צאן קדושים לנחותם הדרך.

כן נזכה כולנו לראות מהרה בתפארת עוזך

ממני הכו"ח בכבוד ובהערצה
בידידות נאמנה
מתתי' חיים סלומן

Table of Contents

Foreword: Words of Encouragement   13
  by HaRav Mattisyahu Salomon

Chapter One:
The Abundant Benefits of Teshuvah

  Day 1: Teshuvah Power   18
  Day 2: Golden Days of Elul   22
  Day 3: Only Teshuvah Can Do It   25
  Day 4: Teshuvah: Damage Undone   29
  Day 5: Hashem's Kindness   33
  Day 6: Keeping His Word   37

Chapter Two:
Coming Closer

  Day 7: Closer Still   42
  Day 8: Teshuvah With Love   46
  Day 9: Reconnecting   51

Chapter Three:
You Can Do It

Day 10: Attempting the Possible   56

Day 11: Lose Battles but Win the War   60

Day 12: In Our Generation   64

Day 13: First, Wake Up   68

Day 14: Serious Intentions   72

Day 15: Destined for Greatness   76

Chapter Four: Strategies for Clearing
the Path to Teshuvah

Day 16: Why Prepare?   82

Day 17: Strategy 1: Going the Right Way   86

Day 18: Strategy 2: Small Steps   90

Day 19: Strategy 3: Increase Yiras Shamayim   94

Day 20: A Father's Message   99

Day 21: Constant Blessings   102

Day 22: For Your Protection   106

Day 23: Strategy 4: Make It Real   109

Day 24: "Fire"   113

Day 25: Strategy 5: Damage Control   117

Day 26: A Public Service   121

Day 27: Productive Fear   125

Day 28: Strategy 6: Study Mussar, Spiritual Ethics   129

Day 29: Effective Mussar   133
Day 30: Strategy 7: Focus on the Negative   138
Day 31: Strategy 8: Accept Responsibility: Who, Me? 141
Day 32: Go With the Flow / No Big Deal   145
Day 33: Strategy 9: Pray / Strategy 10: ASAP   152

Chapter Five:
Techniques to an Enduring Teshuvah

Day 34: Planning for Victory   160
       Technique 1: Treat Causes, Not Symptoms
Day 35: Technique 2: The Power of Resolutions   166
       Make It Work
Day 36: Technique 3:'Ein Bereirah'   173
       Technique 4: Easy Does It
Day 37: Technique 5: Read the Manual   179
       Getting Through
Day 38: Technique 6: Set Safeguards   185
       Technique 7: Take Action
Day 39: Technique 8: Develop Positive Habits   192
       Technique 9: Keep a Journal
Day 40: Technique 10: Visualize Success   198

Halachos: The Laws of Teshuvah

Laws I: Levels of Teshuvah   204
Laws II: Step One on the Road to Teshuvah   208

Laws III: That Lingering Odor   212
Laws IV: Never Again   215
Laws V: Defining "Never"   218
Laws VI: Viduy / Verbal Confession   221
Laws VII: Laws of Verbal Confession   225
Laws VIII: The Final Hurdle   229
Laws IX: Repair Character Flaws   233
Laws X: Middos Make the Man   236
Laws XI: Asking Forgiveness   238
Laws XII: Asking Forgiveness: The Laws   242

Acknowledgments   247

Foreword:

Words of Encouragement

by HaRav Mattisyahu Salomon[1]

*D*uring the war years, the Mirrer Yeshivah escaped to Shanghai, China; it was the only yeshivah to remain intact. The whole world was in flames, and the men in the yeshivah knew that their families at home in Europe were in the gravest danger. When Yom Kippur came, one can well imagine the mood of the yeshivah and the intensity of the prayers.

Shanghai is a humid place, and on that Yom Kippur, it was so hot, so suffocatingly hot that the men, perspiring profusely, prayed in their shirtsleeves, a liberty unheard of in the strict decorum of the Mirrer Yeshivah. People fainted from the heat

---

1. Adapted from *With Hearts Full of Faith* pp. 102-105 (ArtScroll / Mesorah Publications, 2002).

and exhaustion, but the prayers continued with undiminished intensity. So much was at stake.

Against the eastern wall in the front of the yeshivah stood R' Chatzkel Levenstein, the Mashgiach, in his long black caftan and his tallis over his head, impervious to the heat and humidity. As was his custom every Yom Kippur, he took a very long time with each *Shemoneh Esrei*, concentrating on every word with all his strength, as if he bore the weight of the entire Jewish people on his frail shoulders. And so he spent just about the entire day standing, going from one *Shemoneh Esrei* almost directly into the next.

The men of the yeshivah were very moved by the sight of the holy sage, their revered and beloved spiritual leader, praying with such intensity and so oblivious of his surroundings, and they wanted to do something for him, something that would mean a lot to him. And so they had an idea.

After Maariv was over, R' Chatzkel was, of course, still saying the *Shemoneh Esrei*, and everyone knew that it would be a while before he finished. They decided to say Havdalah quickly, have a bite just to break their fast, and come back to the *beis midrash* to learn. When R' Chatzkel finished his *Shemoneh Esrei*, he would turn around and see the whole yeshivah learning the holy Torah, and he would be pleased.

A few minutes after all the students were in place, R' Chatzkel turned around and saw them, and he smiled with pure delight. With tears in his eyes, he addressed his beloved students.

"My precious children," he began, "Let me tell you something. I felt that the prayers of the yeshivah this Yom Kippur were higher and purer than those of any year before. And the repentance was sincere and complete. It was a very special day, an extraordinary day. But I know that some of you are thinking to yourselves that this moment of inspiration will pass. Tomorrow will not be Yom Kippur, and we will slip back from this high place onto which we have climbed today. So did we accomplish? What was the use? Let me tell you a story.

"There was once a man who built himself a beautiful mansion, a real palace. It took a long time to build, and he decided to make a celebration in honor of the completion of the construction, during which he himself would place an extravagant ornament on the pinnacle of the roof. He invited all his friends and family to participate, and in full view of them all, he climbed up to the roof to affix the ornament to his mansion. Just then, a sudden gust of wind blew him off the roof. He dropped the ornament and tumbled to the ground. Dazed and rolling around in agony, he cried out, 'Oy, my mansion has fallen down. My mansion has fallen down. All my work was for nothing.' His friends and family rushed over and reassured him, 'Your mansion hasn't fallen down. You have. You may have broken bones. You may have to go to the hospital. But when you recover, the mansion will still be there. You'll be able to go into it. It hasn't fallen down.'"

"My dear children, we built a mansion this Yom Kippur. Every prayer we offered up is like a different room, and all together we have constructed a beautiful mansion. If tomorrow we feel that we've lost some of our inspiration, I want you to know that the mansion has not fallen down. It will be we who have fallen down. The mansion will still be standing. It will stand forever. One day, we will enter that mansion once again. When and how, that depends on us, but the mansion will always be there waiting for us. It will be there forever."

R' Chatzkel's words of encouragement to his students in the heat of a world war are an important lesson to all of us. When we stand in the synagogue on Yom Kippur to do teshuvah, the thought can sometimes be so intimidating that we may lose heart. We know that it will take so much emotional and spiritual effort to reach the lofty level of teshuvah to which we aspire. Will we be successful? And even if we are, will we be able to maintain ourselves on that high level? Or will we fall back to earth, so to speak? And if we do, is all the effort worthwhile?

The answer is, yes, most definitely yes. All the effort is indeed very worthwhile, because each and every step we take on the road to teshuvah builds us a beautiful mansion. And no matter what happens, that mansion will endure forever.

The Abundant
Benefits of Teshuvah

Teshuvah Power

One Erev Rosh Hashanah, Rav Dessler shared with his students a lasting lesson he had learned as a child. His father, in an effort to help him recognize the actual impact of the judgment of the Yamim Noraim, told him to think about all the disappointments, anguish, setbacks, and difficulties of the year just ended. "These were the direct result of last Rosh Hashanah's decree," Rav Dessler's father explained. "And we are about to be judged again on Rosh Hashanah with the power to prevent them from happening."

Rav Dessler then concluded. "My father said to me, 'You are young. Tuck away this inspiration into your heart. There will come a time when you will be able to actually affect the verdict of the Yamim Noraim.'"[1]

---

1. *Michtav MeEliyahu, Rosh Hashanah*, Vol. 1, p. 27.

*T*hroughout the year Hashem stands ready to accept the teshuvah of those who repent with a full heart to ensure a good judgment. For those of us who have not yet availed ourselves of this opportunity, the ten golden days between Rosh Hashanah and Yom Kippur are especially propitious for that purpose as the prophet Yeshayah states, "*Dirshu Hashem behimatz'o kera'uhu b'heyoso karov,* Seek God when He can be found, call upon Him when He is near."[2] His presence is so near as to be almost palpable.

To fully prepare, we have been granted the entire month of Elul. It is the ideal time when the efforts we expend in self-examination and self-improvement bring us the greatest return. It is the time for maximizing the opportunity to prepare to do teshuvah, to turn the judgment of Rosh Hashanah and Yom Kippur into one for life, happiness, and blessings.

"*Zachreinu l'chaim Melech chafeitz bachaim, v'chasveinu b'sefer hachaim l'maancha Elokim Chaim,* Remember us for life, O King Who desires life, and inscribe us in the Book of Life — for Your sake, O Living God." These words, recited from Rosh Hashanah through Yom Kippur, are not just a request for a renewed lease on life itself; they are all-encompassing.[3] Our prayer for "life" entails good health, a respectable livelihood, increased spirituality, marriage, children, peace in the world, freedom. Each and

---

2. *Yeshayah* 55:6. See *Rosh Hashanah* 18a, which states that this actually refers to the *Aseres Yemei Teshuvah;* see also *Meiri, Chibbur HaTeshuvah,* p. 250.
3. *Ohr Yechezkel, Elul, Yamim Noraim,* p. 109.

every gift that illuminates our lives and strengthens our connection to the spiritual Source of all life are included in "*Zachreinu l'chaim*," our request for life.

> *When special-operations forces undertake a life-or-death mission, they go through arduous, unrelenting preparations. Attention to detail is imperative. They rehearse every foreseeable possibility to ensure that they achieve their mission and come out alive.*

For us, approaching the Yamim Noraim is no less exacting a mission. The Torah teaches that the days between Rosh Hashanah and Yom Kippur are a precious commodity; each can help change our lives for the better as Hashem lovingly awaits our teshuvah. Returning to God on our own accord, out of sincere regret for our departures from His service, and forsaking the sins of the past, ensures that our teshuvah will be accepted and our past sins forgiven.

If we take advantage of the opportunity, relishing the chance we are given to merit a year of happiness and success, we too will have availed ourselves of the power of teshuvah, thereby ensuring a year of success.[4]

---

4. See *Michtav MeEliyahu*, Vol. 5, p. 295, which states that Hashem will reveal the "light" of Mashiach and those within whom there remains even a hairsbreadth of holiness will then awaken to do teshuvah.

Points to Ponder:

- *The 40 days of Elul through Yom Kippur are especially desig-nated by Hashem as a time when teshuvah is most accessible and accepted.*

- *Our fates for the coming year, in all aspects of life, are determined on Rosh Hashanah and sealed on Yom Kippur.*

- *Applying our efforts to sincere teshuvah during these days is a fateful mission, and an opportunity that no one can afford to ignore.*

Golden Days of Elul

Ever since our journey through the Wilderness after the exodus from Egypt, the period from Rosh Chodesh Elul until Yom Kippur has been an *eis ratzon*, an extraordinary time of favor that is especially charged with Divine compassion.[1]

Our first poignant experience with Elul's power to bring us to repentance and forgiveness took place after the egregious sin of the Golden Calf. There we were, fallen from the exalted status we had attained when we accepted the Torah on Mount Sinai, teetering on the verge of oblivion. God was prepared to eradicate us and start anew with Moshe Rabbeinu.[2]

Then, on Rosh Chodesh Elul, Moshe ascended the mountain to accept the Second Tablets of the Covenant. He remained there

---

1. See *Mishnah Berurah,* Introduction to *Siman* 581. See also *Chayei Adam, Klal* 138; *Kitzur Shulchan Aruch* 128:1.
2. *Shemos* 32:10.

pleading day and night with God to forgive His foolish, wayward nation.[3] At last, on Yom Kippur, God forgave the Jewish people and we were restored to our lofty position as His emissaries on earth.[4] From then on, for all eternity, these days have been designated as an *eis ratzon* — a favorable time — for achieving forgiveness.

Elul is the time Hashem gives us to prepare to acquire a clean slate upon which the upcoming year's blessings can be written, and to rally a fresh enthusiasm to fuel our growth.

The shofar, sounded from the first day of Elul through Rosh Hashanah, is our reminder to ready ourselves to be inscribed for a positive judgment in the year to come. Its primary purpose is to awaken us from our spiritual "slumber."[5]

Throughout the year, a person who seeks this renewal must stretch himself to the maximum, at which point he merits Hashem's help to complete the task. During Elul, however, Hashem is ready to "descend" and dwell among us, in "easy reach" of anyone who turns to Him in sincere teshuvah. This is evidenced by the Hebrew letters of the word *Elul* (*aleph, lamed, vov, lamed*), an acronym for the words: *ani ledodi v'dodi li* — I am my Beloved's and my Beloved is mine.[6]

A successful businessman knows that procrastinating, avoiding the difficult tasks and leaving things to chance, spell failure

3. Ibid. 34:2 with *Rashi* to 33:11.
4. *Rashi* ibid.
5. *Rambam, Hilchos Teshuvah* 3:4.
6. *Shir HaShirim* 6:3. However, see *Ohr Gedalyahu, Moadim*, p. 5.

for his enterprise. Teshuvah, the key to a new year of life, cannot be frittered away by poor business practices.

Elul is literally the time for "getting down to business." As the verse[7] states: "If you will seek it as [if it were] silver … then you will understand fear of Heaven." There is no question that a person should treat his service to Hashem with the seriousness and persistence he would apply to acquiring wealth.[8]

Points to Ponder:

- *The days of Elul are charged with especially potent Divine compassion.*

- *Because of its unique nature, it is a propitious time for one to prepare to do teshuvah and gain forgiveness.*

- *Using the power of Elul to its maximum affords the ideal opportunity to be granted a favorable judgment.*

---

7. *Mishlei* 2:4-5.
8. *Chofetz Chaim, Zechor L'Miriam*, Ch. 5, p. 14; *Chovas HaShemirah*, Ch. 8, *Os* 15.

Only Teshuvah Can Do It

To create a publicity "buzz," a local radio station runs a contest that gives the winner 10 minutes' access to a bank vault, where he is allowed to carry off all the cash he can grab. When the time comes to collect his prize, the winner moves with unprecedented precision, speed, and nonstop energy, his hands flying like perfectly calibrated machines.

We each get our "10 minutes" in the form of the Aseres Yemei Teshuvah, and the prize is far more valuable than money. We have the opportunity to grab health, spiritual strength, happiness, and all the things that bring fulfillment in life. There is one specific key provided to unlock the vault, and that is teshuvah.

The Talmud[1] states that most of us are designated by the name *beinonim*[2] — our mitzvos and sins balance. Therefore, our fates are not finalized until Yom Kippur[3] as Hashem grants us these ten days to ensure our place in the Book of Life through the means of teshuvah.

So then we must wonder: Why is teshuvah alone designated as the mitzvah that ensures a judgment for life?[4] Why wouldn't any mitzvah tip the scale in our favor?[5] The reason is because of teshuvah's unique essence.

> *A king seeks to give his subjects access to him, and personally visits their homes. At one home, the occupant goes about his routine, mowing his lawn and repairing his door hinge while the king stands by. The subject's disregard of the king is in itself an affront worthy of punishment.*

---

1. *Kiddushin* 40b.

2. See *Derech Sichah*, Vol. 2, p. 283, that explains that *beinoni* does not refer to one who has precisely the same number of mitzvos and sins. It refers to one who does both good deeds and sins and is torn between the two rulers of his soul: the good and the evil inclinations. A *tzaddik* is one whose ways are righteous; his heart compels him to perform mitzvos but occasionally he sins. A wicked person is one who is dominated by the evil inclination and whose ways are generally bad, but occasionally he merits to do mitzvos. See also *Sifsei Chaim, Moadim,* Vol. 1, p. 243.

3. *Rosh Hashanah* 16b.

4. *Rambam, Hilchos Teshuvah* 3:3; *Kochvei Or,* Section 5; *Mishnas Rav Aharon,* Vol. 2, pp. 179-180; *Sichos Mussar Maamar* 103, pp. 436; *Sifsei Chaim, Moadim,* Vol. 1, p. 243.

5. However, see *Lechem Mishnah, Hilchos Teshuvah* 2:4; *Derech Sichah,* Vol. 2, p. 286.

Hashem "draws" close to the heart of every Jew during these ten golden days from Rosh Hashanah through Yom Kippur. He offers us the chance to come close to Him with teshuvah, and we must respond. To ignore Hashem and make no attempt to be receptive to His offer of closeness is in itself a sin that cannot outweigh other mitzvos done to gain merit.[6]

> *A band of robbers who were imprisoned dig a tunnel and all but one escape. The next morning the guard finds him in the prison with the tunnel open before him. He hits the robber and says, "You fool, the tunnel is open before you and you didn't run away!" So too, Hashem tells the sinner, "The tunnel [of repentance] is open and you did not repent!"[7]*

Through teshuvah, Hashem gives us the power to reach all the way to His Throne of Glory.[8] Even if one has sinned many times, he can hold onto the belief that Hashem still forgives him, that his teshuvah is effective.[9] Then there is nothing to impede it from reaching the Heavenly Throne and being accepted by our ever-loving God, Who wants to forgive us. That is why the

---

6. *Sifsei Chaim, Moadim*, Volume 1, p. 243, s.v. *V'Tiraitz.*

7. *Koheles Rabbah* 7:15.

8. *Yoma* 86a. See *Maharsha* ibid. s.v. *Ad kisei.*

9. See *Rama, Orach Chaim, Siman* 607:6: "Yom Kippur only atones for penitents who believe in Hashem's atonement, but when someone rebels against Him and thinks in his heart, 'Of what use is this Yom Kippur to me,' it does not atone for him." See also *Rambam, Hilchos Shegagos* 3:10. See *Sifsei Chaim, Moadim,* Vol. 1, p. 285, s.v. *Amnam.*

prophet[10] urges us, "Return, O Israel, unto Hashem your God ..."

Hashem is like a caring parent who never entirely forsakes his child.[11] He will not allow our souls to perish within us,[12] as we say at the end of *"Magen Avraham,"* the first blessing of *Shemoneh Esrei,* Hashem watches over the spark of "Avraham Avinu" in each of us.[13] Each Jew is a beloved child of God, and no matter where he finds himself and how many years or generations have elapsed, he will feel the inexorable pull toward his roots. Even if barely audible, his soul will call to him to initiate the teshuvah process.

Points to Ponder

- *Every mitzvah or sin has the potential to tip the scale of judgment. However, sincere teshuvah ensures inscription in the Book of Life.*

- *Teshuvah is Hashem's offer to us to come close to Him.*

- *Ignoring His offer of closeness is in itself an affront to Hashem.*

---

10. *Hoshea* 14:12.
11. See *Malbim, Yechezkel* 33:11.
12. See *Sifsei Chaim, Moadim,* Vol. 1, p. 27.
13. *Ohr Gedalyahu, Moadim,* p. 29.

To the continued hazlocha of The V'Ani Tefillah Foundation.
For the hatzlocha of our children and the health of our parents.
Yitzchok and Dvorah Kornblau

Teshuvah:
Damage Undone

Entranced by a delicate crystal vase that occupies the center of the dining-room table, little Chaim climbs onto a chair. "No, no, mustn't touch," cautions the maternal voice in his head. "It's so shiny. It sparkles with pretty rainbow colors," responds another voice: this one his own. He leans across the table and reaches for the vase, but as his hand tugs on its rim, it topples and shatters into dozens of jagged pieces.

"Oh, no, I shouldn't have touched it!" he thinks. "I'll never do it again," he vows. "Now I ruined it! Mommy will be so angry." Tears of regret are streaming down his round cheeks when suddenly, the glittering pieces of the vase join together, the water and flowers resume their places, and the puddle on the table dries up.

*I*magine this child's wide-eyed expression of amazement when he sees his damage undone! That, on a cosmic scale, is the reality of the spiritual power of teshuvah: to undo the damage and fill our lives with material and spiritual blessings.

When God was about to create man, the Torah "questioned": "If man should sin and be brought to trial before You, the work of Your hand will be in vain, for he will not be able to endure Your judgment." God replied, "Therefore, I fashioned teshuvah before creating the world."[1] Yet, since the world was created *yeish mei'ayin* — a tangible reality out of nothing — how could anything, let alone teshuvah, exist before creation?[2]

The answer can be understood by analyzing a sin as grave as the first murder ever, of Hevel by Kayin.[3] Kayin did teshuvah for his crime.[4] But his teshuvah did not bring Hevel back to life. Killing is not like robbery, where the stolen item can be returned. By what logic can a previous sin, even one as heinous as murder, be forgiven and erased? Why shouldn't the perpetrator be punished for the damage he has already done?

If someone fully and sincerely repents, then God considers the crime as if it were never committed.[5] Teshuvah turns the *yeish* of the crime into an *ayin*: a negation of an act that

---

1. *Zohar, Bereishis* 134b.
2. Adapted from *Selected Speeches*, Rav Shimon Schwab, CIS Publishers, Abridged Edition, pp. 42-43.
3. *Bereishis* 4:8.
4. *Bereishis Rabbah* 22:13.
5. See *Yoma* 86a.

has already taken place. In this sense, teshuvah was created before the formation of the world because teshuvah returns conditions to where they were before Creation. By its ability to wipe out a past action[6] teshuvah renders the misdeed null and void.

Teshuvah is a totally unique process, in which deeds that have been done can be undone. Since teshuvah "preceded" the natural world, it does not and need not conform to natural law.

One who performs teshuvah demonstrates that he sincerely regrets his actions and at the time he repents feels in his heart that he will never repeat them. God then forgives him and abolishes the misdeed, opening the way for renewed blessings, both material and spiritual.[7] The verse, "For I do not desire the death of the wicked,"[8] is dealing with those who engage in teshuvah.[9]

Many times, we wish we could "rewind" a past episode and act with more wisdom, sensitivity, or caution. This is the essence of the power of teshuvah: a reality that truly defies the natural order, and yet, has been lovingly granted to us as a tool in our hands, to bring blessings to our lives.

---

6. *Mesillas Yesharim*, end of Chapter 4. See *Nefesh HaChaim* 1:12, 2:7 cited in *Sifsei Chaim, Moadim*, Vol. 1, p. 292, s.v. *HaGrach mosif*. See also *Koveitz He'aros, Aggados*, Siman 3.

7. *Yoma* 86b; *Rif* on *Ein Yaakov*, ibid. Since his transgressions can be transferred into sources of merit they earn him the blessings of an extended lifespan, enabling him to live longer. See also *Tzlach* ibid.

8. Cf. *Yechezkel* 18:32.

9. *Niddah* 70b.

Points to Ponder:

- Teshuvah has the power to abolish an act that has taken place.

- Teshuvah was created by God prior to His creation of the universe, therefore it operates outside the realm of natural laws.

Hashem's Kindness

On Yom Kippur, the Kohen Gadol spent the day in intense, physically demanding service to God. He atoned for himself, his family and the nation; he entered the Holy of Holies; he pronounced God's ineffable Name. Each of his actions had to be perfect in performance and intent. His failure to perform his service properly could cost his life, and deny the nation forgiveness for their sins.

It was a day of unrelenting exertion. Yet, when the Kohen Gadol emerged, his beaming countenance was described with superlatives. Among them: "lightning bolts emanating from the radiance of the angels," "the crown that is placed on a king's forehead," and "the graciousness of a bridegroom's face."[1]

---

1. *Piyut* of Yom Kippur Mussaf, s.v. *K'Ohel HaNimtach*.

*I*n the secular world of illusion, joy and concerted effort are often mutually exclusive terms. In the actual world of truth, however, exertion, disappointment — sometimes even desperation — are often the fertile soil from which the deepest joy springs. Teshuvah, from the secular perspective, is a dreary concept bound by emotions such as guilt and regret. From the Jewish perspective, however, teshuvah is the greatest gift God has granted us: to erase our misdeeds and to emerge clean before Him.

Teshuvah is "among Hashem's kindnesses to His creations."[2] Knowing that humans are imperfect, God provided us with a way to save ourselves from the consequences of our misdeeds. In fact, as the prophet assures us,[3] even if one makes the biggest mistake a Jew can make, offending God and rebelling against Him, He does not close the doors of teshuvah.[4]

Everything God does is a kindness, yet singling out teshuvah as a kindness of God may seem redundant. This point is emphasized because we are the beneficiaries of God's kindness, therefore we must do teshuvah with happiness.[5] We should see it as an opportunity to become greater, more complete individuals, even if we have sinned.[6]

---

2. *Shaarei Teshuvah, Shaar* 1, s.v. *Min hatovos.*

3. *Yeshayah* 31:6.

4. *Michtav MeEliyahu*, Vol. 4, p. 75.

5. *Matnas Chelko* on *Shaarei Teshuvah*, p. 9. See ibid. p. 31, where Rav Mattisyahu Salomon asserts that people mistakenly believe that the service of teshuvah requires that one be sad.

6. *Michtav MeEliyahu*, Vol. 4, p. 75.

Once we undertake the teshuvah process, we are likely to find that it is liberating;[7] it releases us from all the negativity in our past and sets us free to reach our full potential. We can compare the effort involved to the medication taken by someone disabled by illness. He does what needs to be done gladly, because he knows that this will restore him to full health and life.

Every mitzvah should be done with happiness;[8] however, the happiness is usually external to the mitzvah.[9] With teshuvah, the mitzvah itself creates happiness when we realize that our sins are forgiven and we fully open the door to receive the abundant benefits of this world as well as of the World to Come.[10]

During the days of Elul and the Aseres Yemei Teshuvah, the gift of teshuvah is before us. We may, however, be inclined to leave the gift in its wrapping, mistakenly believing that it contains nothing other than the struggles of self-examination and self-improvement. But if we grab this gift and open it, we will find that it is exactly what we want and what we need to bring us a new year of life, health, prosperity, and happiness.

Points to Ponder:

- *There is no contradiction between difficulty and joy. In fact,*

---

7. Rav Chaim Volozhin cited in *Sifsei Chaim, Moadim* Vol. 1, p. 303.

8. *Pachad Yitzchak, Shabbos/Succos*, p. 190, *Maamar 9, Os 7.*

9. *Rambam, Hilchos Shofar V'Succah V'Lulav* 8:15.

10. See *Shaarei Teshuvah, Shaar 4, Os 8.*

facing and overcoming difficulty is one of the surest paths to true joy.

- *Teshuvah can be arduous, and yet it is God's greatest gift to us, for it enables us to renew ourselves and our connection to God.*

- *Teshuvah is a gift, and should be done with happiness.*

Keeping His Word

It is estimated that 80 million Americans believe we have been visited by aliens from another planet. Numerous studies show that millions of people believe in ghosts, extrasensory perception, and, of course, alien abductions.

People "believe" in many things. Nonetheless, our unwavering belief in Hashem is a certainty.[1] When the Jewish people saw the sea split to let them pass in safety and then close over the heads of their Egyptian pursuers, the Torah[2] states, "And Israel saw the great hand that Hashem inflicted upon Egypt, and the people feared Hashem, and they believed in Hashem and in Moses, His servant."

---

1. Adapted from *Hearts Full of Faith*, Rabbi Mattisyahu Salomon, ArtScroll/Mesorah, pp. 20-21.
2. *Shemos* 14:31.

Under those circumstances, however, it would seem almost impossible *not* to "believe" in the existence of God. Their "belief" is worthy of mention because it indicates that they believed that God would keep His word. That He is trustworthy, and that, just as He had fulfilled His promise to bring them out of Egypt, He would fulfill every promise He had ever made to their ancestors and would ever make to them for all eternity.

Our "belief" in God encompasses the complete trust in the absolute truth and trustworthiness of God's every word. This level of faith is the foundation that had to be laid before the Jewish people were capable of receiving and embracing God's holy Torah. It is at the core of the covenant between God and Israel.

The Talmud[3] states, "What is the meaning of the word *Amen*? Rabbi Chanina said, 'It is the acronym of the words *Ei-l melech ne'eman*, God, trustworthy King.' " We find that trustworthiness of God's every word is actually used to describe God Himself.

Included among the Torah's trustworthy words is the verse,[4] "Rather, the matter is very near to you — in your mouth and in your heart — to perform it." The *Ramban* teaches that "the matter" is teshuvah, which is near to us at all times and in all places.[5] What is the benefit of teshuvah? The Torah[6] promises: "You shall return and listen to the voice of Hashem … Hashem

---

3. *Shabbos* 119b.

4. *Devarim* 30:14.

5. *Ramban, Devarim* ibid.

6. *Devarim* 30:8-10. Also see ibid. vs. 2-3 and *Yechezkel* 18:32.

will make you abundant in all your handiwork … for good …
when you return to Hashem, your God, with all your heart and
all your soul."

Believing with our entire being that God is trusted to reward
virtue and punish sin is beyond question. There is no doubt: Do
teshuvah and God forgives you and wipes away your misdeeds;
thereby opening the way for blessings of livelihood, health,
marriage and family, inner peace, and a renewed closeness with
God.

Points to Ponder

- *Belief in God is a belief in the absolute trustworthiness of God's
  words.*

- *The Torah assures us that teshuvah is within our ability, near to
  us at all times and in all places.*

- *Hashem promises that if we do teshuvah, He will forgive our sins
  and grant us a life of blessing.*

ר״ח מנחם אב Yahrzeit — לע״נ אלטע חי׳ה מרים רייזל בת ר׳ שלמה ישראל

Coming Closer

Closer Still

The estranged best friends hadn't spoken to each other in over a decade. The insult that caused the rift seemed insignificant in retrospect, and yet too many years had gone by, too many life events not shared, for either to make the first move.

Then, one day, they found themselves seated side by side in the waiting room of a doctor's office. The doctor, a specialist, dealt with serious diseases. Each realized that the other was facing great difficulty.

"So … Ben," Mordy said, as if he were resuming an interrupted conversation. "I guess we can skip the 'how are you?' part, huh?"

It was the same wry sense of humor the two had always shared together, and Mordy hoped it would hit the mark.

"Yeah, skip that," Ben replied with a familiar chuckle. "It's good to see you again."

*I*n the scene above, we would not say that Ben and Mordy have brought their friendship back to its original state of closeness. We would, however, say that they had taken a crucial step, and that the relationship between them was improved because of that step. In the same way, small steps of teshuvah have a value in and of themselves, regardless of whether they lead to complete teshuvah.[1]

The root meaning of *teshuvah* is *shuv* — return.[2] Teshuvah means returning to God,[3] bridging the distance caused by our sins. The essence of teshuvah is derived from the verse,[4] "It is our sins that divide between Me and you."[5] Because teshuvah's essence is expressed primarily by becoming closer to God, any small step that we take in that direction, even one that is incomplete, is a giant stride in the right direction and is pleasing to Him.[6]

While other mitzvos must be performed in their entirety to accomplish their particular spiritual function, teshuvah is different. That is because it is, at its core, a healing process. When a person suffers from a disease, each improvement is valuable. Even if he never recovers completely, the progress he does make is precious to him.

---

1. *Sifsei Chaim, Moadim,* Vol. 1, p. 247, s.v. *U'l'chein.*
2. Ibid., p. 257, s.v. *Mah he.*
3. Ibid.
4. *Yeshayah* 59:2.
5. *Mabit, Beis Elokim, Shaar HaTeshuvah,* Ch. 1, s.v. *V'haratzon.* See *Chavatzeles HaSharon Al HaTorah, Bereishis,* pp. 25-27 for a full discussion.
6. *Mishnas Rav Aharon,* Vol. 2, p. 161; Vol. 4, p. 101, s.v. *V'ha'inyan bazeh.* See also *Derech Sichah,* Vol. 1, p. 616, s.v. *Teshuvah al miktzas.*

In fact, incremental progress in teshuvah is an important source of motivation for further advances. Once we begin to feel an increased sense of God's closeness, our desire to sin becomes commensurately weaker. We do not want to forfeit the new sense of closeness we have just attained, and so we are more resistant to flouting Hashem's commandments.

Hashem's concealment, which we are still experiencing during these days leading into the times of Mashiach, tends to cloud our sense of His nearness. However, there is a way to uncover His hidden "face," and that is by doing teshuvah. This is the foundation upon which everything depends, since teshuvah's power heals all the ills of our soul and of the world.[7]

The gift of teshuvah lies in its ability to nullify our past and to dissolve our prior stains. But the undeniable message of teshuvah is that Hashem desires a loving relationship with us,[8] and as long as we live, and whoever we may be, it is never too late to reestablish the connection. In the words of the *Rambam*:[9] "How great is teshuvah that it brings man close to the *Shechinah* ..." Yesterday he was hateful in the sight of Hashem — despised, forsaken, and repulsive — and today he is beloved, desirable, near, and befriended.

---

7. *Akeidah, Parashas Nitzavim.*
8. *Mabit, Beis Elokim, Shaar 2*, Ch. 1, cited in *Sifsei Chaim, Moadim,* Vol. 1, p. 246.
9. *Hilchos Teshuvah* 7:6.

Points to Ponder:

- *The essence of teshuvah is to come closer to God. Any incremental step in that direction is of significant value.*

- *Teshuvah proves that despite our imperfections, God desires to be close to us.*

ט' אב Yahrzeit — לע"נ הרב מאיר בן הרב ברכי־ה ז"ל
ט' אב Yahrzeit — לע"נ הרב חיים ברוך בן ר' משה אהרון ז"ל
לע"נ קדושי שואה ז"ל

Teshuvah With Love

*I*f teshuvah were able only to undo the damage we have done, and open our lives to Hashem's blessings, that would seem to be miraculous enough. However, it does so much more. It not only erases the misdeed, but also enables our relationship with Hashem to be much closer than ever.[1]

However, not all teshuvah can accomplish this remarkable loving closeness to Hashem. There are two distinct types of teshuvah: *teshuvah mi'yirah*, which is teshuvah from fear of punishment; and *teshuvah mei'ahavah*, teshuvah from love of God.[2]

---

1. See *Pesachim* 54a, *Nedarim* 39b. *Radak* (*Yeshayah* 22:11) states that it appears that teshuvah's purpose is independent of its ability to cleanse one from sin. Teshuvah itself is one of the purposes for which the world was created. The loftiest purpose of teshuvah, which reaches the *Kisei HaKavod*, God's Heavenly Throne of Glory, is to enable one to come close to Hashem, the ultimate purpose of our existence. See also *Daas Torah, Devarim*, p. 155, s.v. *Ro'im*.
2. *Yoma* 86b.

Teshuvah mi'yirah is considered a lesser level of teshuvah, because if not for the punishment, the person would not repent.[3] Such teshuvah can expunge our sins, but it does not bring us into the same loving relationship with Hashem as does *teshuvah mei'ahavah*.[4]

"*Achas sha'alti mei'eis Hashem, osah avakeish. Shivti b'veis Hashem kol yemei chayai* ...One thing I asked of Hashem, this I shall seek: That I dwell in the House of Hashem all the days of my life."[5]

This verse from *L'David Hashem Ori,* recited from the first day of Elul through Shemini Atzeres, encapsulates every Jew's simple but profound yearning to attain that loving relationship.[6] God's Name appears thirteen times in *L'David Hashem Ori*, for during this period, the thirteen gates of *rachamim*, of mercy and compassion, are open to us.

Hashem's Thirteen Attribute of Mercy is limitless, therefore we should never worry or wonder whether our sincere teshuvah will be accepted, thereby bringing forgiveness for our sins and drawing us closer to God.[7] Our teshuvah reaches up to an omnipotent God, Whose compassion has absolutely no limits or boundaries. It is no wonder that teshuvah is considered "among

3. *Mishnas Rav Aharon*, Vol. 2, p. 151.
4. *Sifsei Chaim, Moadim,* Vol. 1, p. 247, s.v. *Ha'shav rak;* p 251, s.v. *K'fi she'bei'arnu;* p. 303, s.v. *B'kach navin.*
5. *Tehillim* 27:4.
6. See *Malbim, Tehillim* 27:1,4.
7. *Bnei Yissaschar, Maamarei Chodesh Tishrei, Maamar 4, Derush* 12.

Hashem's kindnesses to His creations."[8]

Hashem's "Thirteen Attributes of Mercy" bear witness to the many ways in which He awaits our teshuvah. Contemplation of each of the Attributes — "Hashem, Hashem, God, Compassionate (before one sins and after); and Gracious; Slow to anger; Abundant in Kindness and Truth; the Preserver of Kindness for thousands of generations; Forgiver of iniquity, willful sin, and inadvertent sin, and Who absolves" — elicits an awareness of all He has done, does, and will do for us.

God revealed His Thirteen Attributes of Mercy to Moshe Rabbeinu, to place this crucial key to attaining forgiveness in our hands. In giving us all of these tools and opportunities to do teshuvah, Hashem's undeniable message is that He desires a loving relationship with us.[9]

All of this compassion flows to us even though we have utilized the very gifts Hashem gives us to commit sins. He grants us intelligence, strength, vitality, creativity, money, and health, and we use these to pursue our own misguided objectives.[10] Not only do we do this, but we repent, and then do it again. Nevertheless, so deep is Hashem's desire for closeness to us that He continues to wait for the awakening of love that will overflow its banks and carry us to teshuvah.[11]

---

8. *Shaarei Teshuvah, Shaar* 1, *Min hatovos*. See *Michtav MeEliyahu*, Vol. 4, p. 75.

9. *Mabit, Beis Elokim, Shaar* 2, Ch. 1.

10. *Tomer Devorah*, Ch. 1.

11. *Machsheves Mussar, Elul, Yamim Noraim*, p. 137. See *Talmud Yerushalmi, Makkos* 2:5; *Yalkut Shimoni, Yechezkel* 358.

The desire to do *teshuvah mei'ahavah*[12] arises when we realize that we have "disappointed" our beloved Father, and are overwhelmed with a longing to reconnect with Him. This renewed surge of love nullifies the damage that our sins have generated.[13] Thus, intentional sins are not only erased, they are turned into merits.[14]

This lofty level of teshuvah is accessible to each of us, because it emanates from the *pintele Yid,* the indelible spark of Jewishness that embodies the "tzelem Elokim" within the deepest recesses of our souls.[15] This heartfelt penitence has the power to turn willful, premeditated transgressions[16] into mitzvos,[17] thereby completely cleansing the soul and enabling us to obtain the greatest benefit of teshuvah: the joy of coming ever closer to Hashem.

Points to Ponder

- *True teshuvah atones for sin, but its intrinsic purpose is to draw us even closer to Hashem.*

---

12. See *Nefesh HaChaim* 4:31.
13. See *Ruach Chaim* 3:2. See Sifsei Chaim, *Moadim*, Vol. 1. p. 304, s.v. Ach hashav.
14. *Yoma* 86b.
15. Sifsei Chaim, *Moadim*, Vol. 1. p. 248, s.v. Achein kach.
16. See *Me'or Einaim* on *Ha'azinu*, which states that even the worst sins can be forgiven.
17. See *She'eilos U'Teshuvos, Teshuvos V'Hanhagos*, Vol. 2, *Siman* 296, p. 253.

- *Teshuvah mi'yirah erases our sin; teshuvah mei'ahavah turns sins into merits.*

- *One's love and longing to draw nearer to Hashem generates additional merit.*

L'ilui nishmas Tzivia bas Menachem Mendel

Reconnecting

A child goes shopping with his father. While the father selects fruit for Shabbos, the child spies the candy aisle and happily wanders away. As soon as the father finds his son missing, he begins searching the store. The boy, however, is oblivious as he contemplates the beckoning sour sticks and lollipops.

Soon, he tires and thinks about hopping into his car seat and snoozing as his father drives home. His father! Where is he? Suddenly, the child can think of nothing else. He's lost and alone ... and then, he sees his father peering down the aisle in search of him. He runs into his father's arms crying, "Daddy! I found you!"

Like this little boy, we tend to wander away from our Father in pursuit of our hearts' desires. For many of us, this defines our day-to-day life. How, then, can we rise to the level of *teshu-*

vah mei'ahavah and reconnect with Hashem in the brief period between Rosh Chodesh Elul and Yom Kippur?

As in the allegory of the little boy, as soon as we realize our total dependence on God in every aspect of our daily lives, we are overcome with longing. The sins themselves generate the sense of separation, which in turn spurs a reconnection so passionate that the one who does teshuvah is said to reach a level where "even the righteous do not stand." [1]

> *One Yom Kippur a Jewish shepherd boy went to shul. Moved to tears by the solemnity and heartfelt prayers, he asked what was happening. He was told that on this day God sits on His throne and seals the judgment of the world. The boy yearned to join in the prayers. However, he knew not one single word of Hebrew.*
>
> *Determined to give Hashem the best he could offer, he began to whistle the tune he used to gather his flock from the fields. The other congregants were aghast at his lack of decorum, but the Baal Shem Tov silenced their scolding.*
>
> *"Until now," he said, "I felt our prayers being blocked as they tried to reach the heavenly court. This young shepherd's tears and whistling broke through the barrier ... since it was sincere and pure and is an expression of his love for Hashem that came from the depths of his heart."[2]*

---

1. *Berachos* 34b; *Sanhedrin* 99a. See *Sichos R' Shimshon Dovid Pincus, Elul, Yamim Noraim*, p. 342.
2. Adapted from *A Treasury of Chassidic Tales, Rabbi S.Y. Zevin*, ArtScroll, p. 124.

The Talmud[3] teaches that after the destruction of the Temple, "all the gates (through which prayers travel) were closed, except for the Gates of Tears." When our tears represent the purest of our thoughts and longing, those tears move worlds.[4]

When with feeling we cry like children[5] — Our Father, merciful Father, Who acts mercifully, have mercy upon us ... — the mere act of *desiring* to come closer to Hashem merits His help.[6] Hashem then instills the "light of teshuvah" into our hearts, launching our climb toward teshuvah.[7]

Tears of regret and embarrassment are so powerful when they arise from the recognition that our relationship with Hashem is indispensable. One must truly believe that all he has is from Hashem,[8] that his health, livelihood, shidduchim, etc. are entirely in Hashem's hands, that in this era of total helplessness

---

3. *Berachos* 32b.

4. Achieving the ultimate level of *teshuvah mei'ahavah* through tears is alluded to in the verse (*Shemos* 2:6), "And behold a lad (*naar*) was crying." The lad referred to in the verse is the baby Moshe [Rabbeinu]. Immediately thereafter the verse (ibid. 2:7) states, "She took pity on him..." *Zohar* (*Shemos* 12b) explains that when the Jewish people open their hearts to teshuvah through tears, Hashem immediately has mercy upon them.

5. *Michtav MeEliyahu*, Vol. 1, p. 104; Vol. 4, pp. 76-77.

6. See ibid. *Michtav MeEliyahu*, Vol. 1, p. 28; *Sifsei Chaim, Moadim*, Vol. 1, p. 256, s.v. *Ka'amur; Mabit, Sefer Beis Elokim, Shaar HaTeshuvah*, Ch. 1.

7. *Michtav MeEliyahu*, Vol. 1, p. 245; Vol. 4, p. 74. See *Sifsei Chaim, Moadim*, Vol. 1, p. 253, which states that because the baal teshuvah's ascension is only because of *siyata d'Shmaya*, it is limitless. Therefore, the baal teshuvah is said to reach a level upon which "even the righteous cannot stand."

8. *Shabbos* 107b.

and decay we must place our faith on *Avinu shebaShamayim,* our Father in Heaven.[9] When that realization strikes us, it ignites in our soul the spark to do teshuvah. Thus, even the first stirrings of teshuvah in our hearts merit *siyata d'Shmaya,* enabling us to reconnect.[10]

Points to Ponder:

- *Our sins generate a separation from Hashem.*
- *The feeling of separation leads to a strong longing to reconnect.*
- *Hashem helps those who long to return to Him.*

---

9. *Sotah* 49b.
10. *Michtav MeEliyahu,* Vol. 4, p. 74.

May today's learning be a zechus for a refuah sheleimah for
Nechama bas Tziril

CHAPTER
THREE

You Can Do It

Attempting the Possible

Chava looked through the open window onto the backyard. There, she spotted 4-year-old David, standing on a picnic table clutching five helium balloons in his hand. With determination straining his pudgy face, he jumped up and down on the table. Over and over, he jumped, marshaled his energy, and jumped again.

"David, what are you doing?" Chava shouted.

"I'm trying to fly!" he proclaimed.

Had he not believed that five balloons possessed enough lift to carry him aloft, he would no doubt have quit his exhausting experiment after a few tries, if he had indeed tried at all. But he was convinced that it could be done, and therefore, he persisted.

It is our place to know that teshuvah can be done, for without that certainty, there would be no incentive to try. Certainly, there would be no incentive to persist when setbacks arise. However, when there is a vision of success spurring us on, we can strive to do teshuvah, or to pursue any goal.

Success, like failure, is an experience every person has had in several areas of life. Unfortunately, many people allow the failures to overshadow their successes, producing a self-image that is both gloomy and inaccurate. To embark on change we need compelling evidence that we can succeed; otherwise, why try?

The most reliable evidence is past success. When you pull those instances out of the shadows, you see that you have already come a long way: mastered many skills, developed many fine traits, taken upon yourself many important commitments and fulfilled them.

Once you strengthen your belief that you can succeed in general, you still must address your doubts about succeeding in teshuvah. Can you really become better? As we quoted earlier, the Torah guarantees that we can succeed:

> *"For the commandment that I command you today is not hidden from you and it is not distant ... Rather the matter is very near to you — in your mouth and your heart — to perform it."*[1]

---

1. *Devarim* 30:11,14. See *Sforno, Devarim* 30:14, who explains that the heart recognizes where one has sinned and the mouth confesses it.

If teshuvah is "very near," why must the verse also state that "it is not distant"? Chofetz Chaim[2] explains that the evil inclination attempts to tell us that teshuvah is distant. The verse responds, you are being persuaded that teshuvah appears to be 'distant' — far away from us. The truth is, however, that it is 'very near.'

> *Hashem does not ask a person to perform the mitzvah of building a fence around his porch unless Hashem has first given him a house.[3] Hashem does not ask one to wear tzitzis unless he first provides him with a garment.[4]*

Ramban[5] explains that "in your mouth and in your heart — to perform it" confirms our ready access to teshuvah, for Hashem does not command a mitzvah unless it is beneficial and doable[6] for every Jew.

Our history of personal successes tells us we can do it. The Torah tells us we can do it. Indeed, Hashem helps those who desire and who make an effort to repent.[7] Armed with the belief

---

2. Cited in *Derech Sichah,* Vol. 1, p. 614.

3. *Devarim* 22:8; *Chinuch, Mitzvah* 546.

4. *Vayikra Rabbah* 27:2.

5. *Devarim* 30:14.

6. See *Michtav MeEliyahu,* Vol. 4, p. 23, where Rav Dessler comments that no person is given tests that are too difficult: "All that [Hashem] gives a person in this world, whether intelligence or wealth, are tests for him, to see whether he will become haughty and will take it [intelligence or wealth] for himself or whether he will use it to serve God. However, see *Tzidkas HaTzaddik, Os* 43.

7. *Shaarei Teshuvah, Shaar* 1, *Siman* 1. See *Sefer Sifsei Chaim,* Vol. 1, p. 13.

that success is within our reach, we can open ourselves to our souls' innate longing for Hashem, and fearlessly take the first small step forward.

Points to Ponder:

- *One embarks on change only when he feels it is possible to succeed.*

- *The Torah does not command that which is impossible, therefore success in teshuvah is attainable.*

May today's learning be a zechus for a refuah sheleimah for
Chaya Avivia bas Rochel

Lose Battles but Win the War

A person is willing to put in effort in order to reach a goal. If that goal seems to keep slipping out of his grasp, he eventually loses his will to try. It is this frustration Rav Hutner[1] addresses in the following powerful letter to a student:

> *When we tell stories of a gadol (great person), we only record their later years, when they have already become gedolim, and we make it sound as if they were perfect from birth. Rather ... realize that the greatness that the gedolim have achieved results from a steady, tenacious war against every base inclination ...*

---

1. *Igros Pachad Yitzchak*, Number 128.

Everyone is amazed at the purity of speech of the Chofetz Chaim, but who knows of the ... battles, obstacles, slumps, and regressions that the Chofetz Chaim encountered in his war with the yetzer hara? ...

Certainly, you have stumbled and will stumble again, and in many battles you will fall. I promise you, though, that after those losing battles, you will emerge victorious ... Lose battles but win wars.

What does God want from us when we sin? He wants us to do teshuvah.[2] Teshuvah means returning to the path God set for us when we were born, the path that our souls recognize as homeward bound, the path of goodness, of becoming a better person, a different person,[3] not a *perfect* person.[4]

Imagine a young child taking his first steps in front of the proud parents. He gets to his feet, takes a few steps, and falls flat on his face. The parents clap with joy. But if you analyze the scenario, shouldn't the parents be upset? After all, the child fell down!

King Solomon[5] said, "For though a righteous one may fall seven times [in spiritual matters], he will arise, but the wicked

---

2. The word Teshuvah is often inaccurately translated as repentance.
3. Alter of Slabodka, Cited in *Tehillim Treasury,* ArtScroll/Mesorah Publ., p. 205; *Ohr Gedalyahu, Moadim,* p. 17.
4. *Pathways of the Prophets, Rabbi Yisroel Reisman,* ArtScroll/Mesorah, p. 118.
5. *Mishlei* 24:16.

ones will stumble through evil." This verse teaches that in order to become a righteous person, one must fall again and again, and keep getting up. Through the process of falling and rising again, a person becomes a *tzaddik*.[6]

Enduring change is a process. It often involves taking two steps forward and one step back. We must come to the realization that a step back is to be regarded as a learning experience and not as a sign of failure. It is through this process that we eventually succeed.

Feeling discomfort, discontent, or disappointed is often the catalyst for us to make great strides. These unpleasant emotions propel us to take steps to seek to better our lives.

For us, the key is the belief that we will succeed in our desire to change. God doesn't expect us to make changes that are as yet beyond our reach. It is out of God's love for us that He provides this method of getting back on track.[7] Once we have taken steps in the right direction, God accepts our return.

Points to Ponder:

- *A step back should not be perceived as failure but as a learning process.*

---

6. Baal Shem Tov, cited in *Pathways of the Prophets*, Rabbi Yisroel Reisman, ArtScroll / Mesorah p. 47.

7. Ramchal, *Mesillas Yesharim*, Ch. 4; *Rabbeinu Yonah*, the opening line of *Shaarei Teshuvah*.

- *The words of King Solomon teach that it is the willingness to keep rising and trying after the fall that builds one into a tzaddik.*
- *All God expects is that we move in the right direction.*

In Our Generation

The Olympic spectators gasped as the pole vaulter planted his long, thin pole into the ground and thrust himself into the air, soaring over the 20-foot-high bar and landing neatly on the other side. They were witnessing the setting of a new record in an Olympic contest that began with the ancient Greeks.

In all those years, the bar has gradually inched upward. The higher standards are the result of improved equipment and training, and the human urge to compete and surpass.

Spiritually, however, the world's "bar" has been sliding downward with each new generation. Nevertheless, when we clear our generation's bar, even if it is a few short inches off the ground, we win the gold. We cannot reach the heights of the previous generations, but we are not expected to do so.[1]

---

1. See *She'eilos U'Teshuvos, Teshuvos V'Hanhagos*, Vol. 4, *Siman* 148, p. 136, s.v. *Bizmaneinu*.

The heightened awareness of Elul and Aseres Yemei Teshuvah are not intended to break our hearts and to have our souls give up ... Hashem does not ask more than what a person can do. What does Hashem want from us? He desires teshuvah that is consistent with our abilities and strength.[2]

Not only are we not expected to perform to the level of the earlier generations, we must realize that *because* the spiritual standing of our generation is so small, our minuscule accomplishments far outweigh those of prior generations.[3] Just as a few wobbly steps by a toddler suffice to win his parents' accolades, so do our wobbly steps toward Hashem bring Him to open "His arms," so to speak, with love.[4]

> *Rabbeinu Yonah states in the name of the Raavad that one who leaves over a little food in his plate at the end of a meal in order to overcome his desire for food is considered to have fasted many fasts. And that was in the Raavad's generation.[5] Imagine how significant this is in our generation.[6]*

The truth is that regardless of a person's spiritual standing, everything a Jew does is important in the Heavenly scheme.

---

2. Said in the name of Rav Yechezkel Levenstein, the Ponovezh Mashgiach, *Aleinu L'Shabei'ach, Devarim, Parashas Nitzavim*, p. 284.
3. *She'eilos U'Teshuvos, Teshuvos V'Hanhagos*, Vol. 4, *Siman* 148, p. 136, s.v. *Bizmaneinu*.
4. *Aleinu L'Shabei'ach, Vayikra*, Introduction, p. 16.
5. Twelfth Century C.E.
6. *Aleinu L'Shabei'ach, Vayikra*, Introduction, p. 19.

As the *Nefesh HaChaim*[7] explains:

> *A Jew should never think to himself, "What difference can my insignificant actions make?" On the contrary, how exalted are his actions, each one reaching up ... to have its impact in the highest heights, in the spiritual worlds and the splendorous lights above!*

There is a well-known Mishnah[8] that states that each person should think, "*Bishvili nivra ha'olam* — The world was created for me."[9] Each newborn is like the lead actor walking onto the stage precisely on cue to play his part. If he misses his cue or stands in the wings crippled by stage fright, the play will not unfold as it should. Each individual's unique role is essential in completing God's creation and in glorifying His Name.

Points to Ponder

- *Our teshuvah and spiritual growth is measured in light of our own generation.*

- *Because of the spiritual weakness of today, even the smallest steps are highly valued by Hashem.*

---

7. Section 1, Ch. 4.
8. *Sanhedrin* 37a.
9. See *Ohr Gedalyahu, Bereishis*, p. 15.

- *Every person in every generation has his unique role to play in glorifying Hashem's Name.*

May today's learning be a zechus for a refuah sheleimah for
Yitzchok ben Rifka Malka
Dedicated by The V'ani Tefillah Foundation

First, Wake Up

A talmid chacham once came to the Chazon Ish and lamented, "Every year, I prepare to do teshuvah. But what is all this worth if right after Yom Kippur I revert to my old habits? The Chazon Ish replied, "Hirhur teshuvah (thoughts of teshuvah) are also very precious to Hashem![1]

oes teshuvah actually have a shortcut,[2] as the concept of *hirhur teshuvah* seems to imply? Does a simple awakening of the heart satisfy the requirements[3] of complete teshuvah, including regret, forsaking one's sin, and verbal confession?[4]

---

1. *Aleinu L'Shabei'ach, Vayikra, Parashas Emor,* p. 445.
2. See *Michtav MeEliyahu,* Vol. 1, p. 30, s.v. *B'eis noraah.*
3. *Rambam, Hilchos Teshuvah,* Ch. 2:2.
4. See *Minchas Chinuch, Mitzvah* 364. See also *Takanas HaShavim,* beginning of *Siman* 9.

Every day, a heavenly voice cries out "Return, children, return."[5] Although we cannot hear the heavenly voice, our *neshamah*, the spiritual spark within us that emanates from God,[6] "hears" the voice that awakens our heart, causing the *hirhur teshuvah* that we experience.[7] Thus, *hirhur teshuvah* represents an awakening from spiritual slumber, without which teshuvah cannot occur.[8] It is a beginning, and a valid one, for it sets in motion a cycle of heightening spiritual awareness. The awakening leads to a small elevation: a crack in the armor of defilement that surrounds the heart,[9] which in turn leads to the potential for complete teshuvah.[10]

Each year, the Jewish calendar features one Yom Tov devoted to *hirhur teshuvah*. Even though Rosh Hashanah is a Day of Judgment, and the first of the Ten Days of Repentance, there is no *Viduy* nor any mention of specific sins in the prayers.[11] Before teshuvah can occur, there must be a spontaneous, heartfelt awakening.[12] The shofar is the "alarm clock," which calls out,

---

5. *Zohar,* Vol. 3, p. 126a, cited in *Nesivos Shalom,* Vol. 1, p. 211.

6. See *Bereishis* 1:26-27 which states that every person is created in the image of God, *tzelem Elokim.*

7. Baal Shem Tov, cited in *Nesivos Shalom* ibid; *Sifsei Chaim, Moadim,* Volume 1, p. 278, s.v. *Nimtzeinu.*

8. *Sifsei Chaim, Moadim,* Volume 1, p. 277, s.v. *Biglal.*

9. *Michtav MeEliyahu,* Vol. 2, p. 44.

10. Ibid., Vol. 4, p. 75.

11. See *Kovetz Sichos Maamar Mordechai,* Vol. 1, pp. 6-10; *She'eilos U'Teshuvos, Teshuvos V'Hanhagos,* Vol. 2, *Siman* 296, p. 253, and see *Sefer Sifsei Chaim, Moadim,* Volume 1, p. 263, s.v. *Gam* for an additional explanation.

12. See *Sifsei Chaim, Moadim,* Volume 1, p. 274, s.v. *Im Kain.*

"Awake, sleepers from your sleep, and slumberers, from your slumber ..."[13]

> One such instance was recounted regarding the tzaddik Reb Leib Sarah, a disciple of the Baal Shem Tov. He had arrived in a village shortly before Yom Kippur to find that there were only eight Jews, not enough for a minyan. "Perhaps we could find a Jew who left the fold," suggested the tzaddik. "The doors of repentance are not locked, even for an apostate."
>
> One villager spoke up. "There is an apostate here: the squire who owns the village. But he has been mired in sin for 40 years."
>
> The tzaddik approached the squire and pleaded, "Tonight is Yom Kippur. Please be the tenth man of the minyan."
>
> The squire acquiesced. Throughout Yom Kippur, the squire stood in shul, humbled and contrite. At the climax of Ne'ilah, when the minyan recited in unison, "Hashem Hu HaElokim, Hashem only He is God," for the seventh time, the squire sighed deeply and his soul departed.
>
> The tzaddik said,[14] "There are those who in one hour earn their portion in the World to Come."

No matter what one's situation, there is no point in standing still, wondering what to do. One must take the first step[15] and the rest will follow.

---

13. *Rambam Hilchos Teshuvah* 3:4.
14. Adapted from *A Treasury of Chassidic Tales, Rabbi S.Y. Zevin*, ArtScroll, p.127.
15. See *Michtav MeEliyahu*, Vol. 4, pp. 108-109.

Points to Ponder

- *Hirhur teshuvah is the first crucial step, in which a person's soul hears heaven's call to awaken.*

- *Even when it causes only a slight shift away from sin, hirhur teshuvah can have a powerful impact on a person's soul.*

L'ilui nishmas Leiby Kletzky
hayeled Yehuda ז"ל ben יבלח"ט Nachman
whose legacy has inspired so much goodness
Dedicated by the V'ani Tefillah Foundation

Serious Intentions

As an infant, Yehoshua ben Chananyah's mother would bring his cradle to the study hall every day so that his ears would absorb the Torah being learned there. Eventually, he became one of the greatest Talmudic Sages of his generation. His mother knew that it wasn't the occasional, dramatic event that would form her child's character; rather, it was the small things, done consistently, which would shape his spiritual identity and determine his future.[1]

*W*ith rare exceptions, all great achievements begin with small steps, and proceed through persistence and consistency. Teshuvah is no exception. The first small step we take constitutes a true breakthrough and a new beginning.

---

1. *Talmud Yerushalmi, Yevamos* 1:6.

When we purchase a house or a car, we give a deposit to reserve our option to buy. How can a seller accept a small amount, perhaps just $500, as adequate incentive to hold the car for us? How can the seller of a house accept just 10 or 15 percent of the price of his home as sufficient to withdraw it from the market?

The deposit money is indeed a mere fraction of the entire amount that will be paid when the deal goes through. It is enough, however, to signal that we are serious. It is too significant an amount to forfeit, and so the seller accepts. Thus, that small amount changes reality, putting us in a completely different position than we would have been in had we not made the deposit.[2]

In the same way, our first small step toward Hashem changes the situation far more than would seem possible. We have major strides to take, and yet, we do something small, and based on that, everything is different. We have reversed direction and come closer — even one small step closer — to Hashem. We have embarked on the road to complete *teshuvah*, the most meaningful journey of our lives.

> *Today, Atlanta, Georgia has a Jewish community that boasts all the basic amenities of a flourishing frum community: a cheder, Bais Yaakov, a kollel, a mikveh; you name it, they have it. But when Rabbi Emanuel Feldman became the rabbi in the late*

2. As heard from Rabbi Yisroel Reisman.

1950's, there was not even one minyan of Shabbos-observant Jews. The Yom Kippur after assuming his post, Rabbi Feldman spoke to the congregants, and said, "I want everyone in this room to keep one thing, for one year."

If the thriving religious community in Atlanta was built on baby steps toward Hashem, then we can certainly build our teshuvah in that manner.

A man once complained bitterly to Rav Yecheskel Levenstein that he was unable to do teshuvah. The Mashgiach told him, "Start by being careful of what you look at on just one street." The man returned to say that he was unable to do even that. The Mashgiach implored him, "Be careful only at the beginning of the street, and with that you will eventually succeed."[3]

There is no such thing as a step toward Hashem that is insignificant. We can never lose by trying; we can only lose by standing still. Each millimeter closer brings us infinite reward and strength for the next step.

Points to Ponder

- *One small step toward teshuvah changes our status.*

---

3. *Kovetz Sichos Maamar Mordechai,* Vol. 1, p. 87, s.v. *Kibalti.*

- *Even the smallest change is worthwhile.*

- *Lasting progress in spiritual matters is effected through consistent, small steps.*

May today's learning be a zechus for
Serach Deena ע"ה bas יבלח"ט Shalom Dovid
Dedicated by Rosenblum / Friedman / Elman / Kleinman families

Destined for Greatness

In the course of traveling to sell his works, the Chofetz Chaim entered an inn in Vilna. A burly man picked up an entire roasted hen and stuffed it into his mouth, washing it down with a gulp of beer that left the stein nearly empty.

Upon learning that the man had been kidnaped as a child by the Russian army, the Chofetz Chaim walked over to the former soldier and shook his greasy hand. "I heard that you actually survived the army of Czar Nikolai and you remained a steadfast Jew! I only wish that I would be guaranteed a place like yours in the World to Come. You have withstood harsher tests than the sages of old!"

The soldier looked up from his plate with tears in his eyes. He leaned over and kissed the hand of the elderly sage. Then the Chofetz Chaim continued. "I am sure that if you get yourself a teacher and continue your life as a true Torah-observant Jew, there will be no one in this world more fortunate than you!"[1]

*L*ike the soldier in the above story, people are subjected to tremendously difficult tests in their lives. Yet we can draw the strength to meet these challenges from the knowledge that God does not impose trials that are beyond our capacity.[2]

In fact, when we take a step in the right direction, Hashem gives us what we need to ultimately succeed.[3] "One who comes to purify himself (*ba l'taheir*) receives *siyata d'Shmaya* — Divine assistance,[4] and without Divine assistance it is impossible to withstand the evil inclination."[5] As the Talmud[6] states, "In the way that a person wants to go, he will be led."

Every Jew can achieve spiritual greatness.[7] In every *nisayon*, we can choose whether we will search out Hashem's will or follow the dictates of other forces, such as greed, pleasure, social

---

1. According to Rabbi M. M. Yasher, biographer of the Chofetz Chaim, the soldier became a pupil of the Chofetz Chaim, and eventually became an outstanding *tzaddik* (righteous Jew).
2. *Ramban, Bereishis* 22:1. *Rav Chaim Shmulevitz, Sichos Mussar, Maamar* 21, s.v. *S'chor s'chor*, p. 91, s.v. *U'ma she'matzinu.*
3. See *Ohr Gedalyahu, Shemos,* p. 68, s.v. *Nekudah,* and *Michtav MeEliyahu,* Vol. 1, p. 222, s.v. *U'b'maamar.*
4. *Yoma* 38b; *Rambam, Hilchos Teshuvah* 6:5.
5. *Kiddushin* 30b. See *Divrei Yoel,* Vol. 3, *Shemos,* p. 44 who explains why Hashem created the evil inclination this way.
6. *Makkos* 10b.
7. *Rambam, Hilchos Teshuvah* 5:1.

pressure, or status-seeking.[8] If we are sent a specific challenge, that is a sign that we are able to withstand it and achieve greatness — a heightened spiritual level coming closer to Hashem,[9] and eternal reward — by passing that test. All Heavenly trials are for the benefit of those being tested.[10]

> *Greatness does not happen by chance. Our paradigm for spiritual greatness — our forefathers — illustrates that it is the product of a purposeful method. What is that method? What made our forefathers great? It was Heavenly test after Heavenly test, [which led to] growth after growth — the impetus for their growth and development were the Heavenly tests.* [11]

As *Mesillas Yesharim*[12] teaches:

> *All that occurs in this world is to test man … there is no one that Hashem does not test. The wealthy individual — he is tested whether his hand will be open to poor people. And the test for the poor person is whether he can accept the afflictions of poverty and not become angry [at God].*

When challenges arise, it is as if a heavenly spotlight suddenly shines on you, and a voice announces, "You're on!" It

---

8. See *Sichos Mussar, Maamar* 91, *Darchei Hayetzer,* p. 386.
9. *Sifsei Chaim, Moadim,* Vol. 1, p. 249, s.v. *lamadnu.*
10. *Ramban, Devarim* 13:4; *Sforno* ibid.
11. *Bereishis Rabbah* 55:1, cited in *Kovetz Sichos Maamar Mordechai,* Vol. 2, p. 168, s.v. *K'var dibarnu.*
12. Chapter 1.

is your opportunity to perform to your best ability, to make a name for yourself in Heaven that will shine for eternity.[13]

Points to Ponder:

- *Nisyonos — spiritual tests — are designed to bring out that potential.*

- *When a person faces a challenge and makes his choice based on God's will, he passes the test and ascends to a greater spiritual level.*

- *This is true no matter where on the ladder a person starts.*

---

13. See *Daas Torah on Bereishis*, end of p. 292. See Rambam, *Moreh Nevuchim* 3:24; *Sichos Mussar*, *Ma'amar* 11, *Midas Hahistaglus*, p. 47.

May today's learning be a zechus
לע״נ Avraham Tzvi ben Dovid ז״ל

CHAPTER FOUR

Strategies for Clearing the Path to Teshuvah

Why Prepare?

In the early 1990's, a research study of violin students from the Academy of Music in Berlin indicated that the best violin students had spent approximately 10,000 hours practicing; the good students had practiced for about 8,000 hours, and the mediocre ones about 4,000 hours. 10,000 hours equals 20 hours a week for 10 years.[1]

Nothing of value is achieved without preparation.[2] For us to achieve our highest hopes as Hashem seals our fate on Yom Kippur, each of us needs to actively prepare.[3]

---

1. *Mishpacha*, Jewish Family Weekly, "Cache of the Day," Issue 362, 3 Sivan 5771/ June 5, 2011, p. 117.
2. See *Kedushas Levi, Parashas Beshalach,* s.v. *Vayomer Hashem el Moshe*, which states that certainly, every mitzvah requires careful preparation in order for it to be performed properly.
3. See *Michtav MeEliyahu*, Vol. 5, p. 191.

To succeed at teshuvah, we have to proceed as if we were preparing for a hike through rough mountain terrain. We would never tackle such a grueling trek without preparation, because we understand that the stakes are high. Likewise, those who understand what is truly at risk would never approach that day unprepared.

> *During Elul, R' Itzele Peterburger donned a special garment. Sewn into it were three pockets in which R' Itzele carried the classic mussar works: Shaarei Teshuvah, Chovos HaLevavos, and Mesillas Yesharim — his "arsenal" with which to prepare for the Day of Judgment.*[4]

What, in fact, does it mean to prepare? It means setting in place a plan as to how to advance from our present situation to our ultimate goal. It means gathering the resources we will need to complete our plan, so that we are ready to act. And last but not least, it means taking action – practicing the skills we will need to succeed in our mission. Just as the violinists' virtuosity was perfected with their hours of practice, we too can train ourselves in the fine-tuned art of teshuvah.

For every moment we invest in preparation, we enhance the effectiveness of our effort. "If I had eight hours to chop down a tree, I'd spend six sharpening my ax," Abraham Lincoln once

---

4. *The Manchester Rosh Yeshivah,* Rabbi Shimon Finkelman with Rabbi Yosef Weiss, ArtScroll/Mesorah, p. 265.

said. How are we, as we approach the crucial days of the Yamim Noraim, supposed to "sharpen our ax"? If preparation is the key, how do we prepare?

We need a plan. The *Sfas Emes* wrote that, without doubt, Heaven places a special awakening within people to do teshuvah in these days, and therefore, we have the obligation to make the effort to capitalize on this gift. We do so by adopting and applying the necessary strategies that will motivate us.

By studying the following strategies you will access the keys that best enables you to begin the teshuvah process which in turn will bring you closer to Hashem:

- *Strategy 1:* Going the Right Way
- *Strategy 2:* Small Steps
- *Strategy 3:* Increase *Yiras Shamayim*
- *Strategy 4:* Make It Real
- *Strategy 5:* Damage Control
- *Strategy 6:* Study *Mussar*, Spiritual Ethics
- *Strategy 7:* Focus on the Negative
- *Strategy 8:* Accept Responsibility: Who Me
- *Strategy 9:* Pray
- *Strategy 10:* ASAP – The Future Is Now

Teshuvah is for everyone, including the righteous.[5] Through teshuvah, a person develops his awe and love of God, gradually arriving at an awareness of even the slightest breach of His will.[6]

---

5. See *Sifsei Chaim, Moadim*, Vol. 1, p. 258, s.v. *teshuvah.*

6. *Nesivos Shalom*, Vol. 1, pp. 195-196.

Each person, at his own level, can elevate himself through te-shuvah.[7]

The more we plan, prepare, and practice, the more beautiful our symphony of teshuvah will sound as we seek to merit life and blessing. By applying any or all of these strategies, we can fulfill the blessing of the *Shemoneh Esrei*, "Bring us back, our Father, to Your Torah, and bring us near, our King, to Your service, and influence us to return in perfect repentance before You."

Points to Ponder

- *As in any human endeavor, success in teshuvah is a function of planning, preparation, and practice.*

- *We avail ourselves of time-tested strategies that prepare us for the judgment of Yom Kippur.*

---

7. *Tzidkas HaTzaddik, Os* 67, 134.

Strategy 1:
Going the Right Way

A fire broke out in a high-rise building.

"Take the escape route, now!" an office worker called as he ran past a confused man wandering in the smoke-filled corridor. "There's only one way to get out alive!"

But where was the escape route? Left or right? Which stairwell? Without knowing precisely what he had to do to escape the fire, the man could not benefit from the office worker's advice.

Do teshuvah? Indeed, it is the only way to escape from the spiritual conflagration ignited by sin. On the spiritual level, teshuvah is as urgent as an escape from a blazing building, whose success we would want to ensure to the highest possible degree.

Teshuvah is not a place for random efforts in different directions; it is a place for precise, knowledgeable action. A person who wants to do teshuvah must learn the specific "escape route" that God prepared at the very inception of the world. Only by following that route can we arrive safely at forgiveness and renewal.

The Torah[1] puts forth the commandment of teshuvah with the following words:

> *For this mitzvah that I command you today — it is not hidden from you and it is not distant. It is not in heaven, [for you] to say, "Who will ascend to heaven for us and take it for us, so that we can listen to it and perform it?" Nor is it across the sea, [for you] to say, "Who can cross to the other side of the sea for us and take it for us, so that we can listen to it and perform it?" Rather, the matter is very near to you — in your mouth and in your heart — to perform it.*

The words "this mitzvah"[2] in the above verse refer to teshuvah.[3] For anyone who sins, teshuvah is an obligation akin to other positive mitzvos, such as donning *tefillin*. Teshuvah is defined by specific laws which are as imperative as, for example, the laws of *chametz*.[4] We cannot fulfill the mitzvah unless we act in accordance with our learning.

---

1. *Devarim* 30:11-14.
2. Cf. *Rashi* who understands the section to be referring to accepting all the mitzvos of Torah; *Rambam Hilchos Talmud Torah* 3:8.
3. *Ramban, Devarim* 30:11; *Sforno*, ad loc.
4. *Daas Chochmah U'Mussar*, Vol. 2, *Maamar* 90, p. 308.

To engage in proper teshuvah we must apply our time and effort to study the laws and effectively eradicate the sin. It is not enough to simply "feel badly" and go on with life. Even if we cannot tackle all of our deficiencies at once, Hashem accepts the teshuvah we are able to do and considers it worthy of merit.[5]

It is worthwhile to note that although "Charity saves from death,"[6] it does not substitute for teshuvah.[7] Attempting to achieve the benefit of teshuvah through charity is compared to trying to "bribe" God. This is not effective, because "God ... does not show favor and ... does not accept a bribe."[8] Therefore, even if a person tries to counterbalance his sins by performing other outstanding mitzvos, such as charity, he has not mitigated the sin that distances him from God.[9]

Like a powerful medicine capable of defeating a devastating disease, teshuvah must contain the right measure of the precise

---

5. *Derech Sichah*, Vol. 1, p. 616.

6. *Bava Basra* 10a.

7. *Shaarei Teshuvah, Shaar* 1:47. However, see *Rosh Hashanah* 17a and *Megillah* 28a where *Chazal* teach us, "*Kol hamaavir al midosav, maavirim mimenu kol peshaav,* A person who overlooks wrongdoings against him will have all his sins removed from him."

8. *Devarim* 10:17. In Midrash *Mishlei* 6:32, *Chazal* explain that Hashem does not take bribes to forgive sins. For a further discussion, see *Pathways of the Prophets*, Rabbi Yisroel Reisman, ArtScroll/Mesorah, pp. 189-191, "Are Tradeoffs Accepted in Heaven?"

9. See *Shaarei Teshuvah, Shaar* 1:47 with *Matnas Chelko*, on *Shaarei Teshuvah*, p. 71, where it is explained that there are sins that even after one has done teshuvah still require afflictions to achieve forgiveness. It is in those situations that "charity saves [one] from death" applies. However, in all circumstances teshuvah is necessary.

ingredients. These are contained in the essential halachos of teshuvah which appear in the section at the end of the book **Halachos — The Laws of Teshuvah.**

We urge the reader to review one of these extremely important halachos each day for 12 days. In doing so, we are doing our utmost to ensure that the life-saving medicine for curing our spiritual ills is authentic and full strength.

See Laws I: Levels of Teshuvah (page 204).

Points to Ponder

- *Teshuvah offers a priceless benefit, and therefore, there are criteria that must be met.*

- *There is no way — not even through giving charity — to bypass the requirements of teshuvah.*

Strategy 2: Small Steps

If Ari had $1,000 to give to tzedakah, should he give the entire sum to one recipient, or give $10 to 100 recipients? The more frequent, smaller donations are preferable, because more frequent giving reinforces our self-image as "givers."

This is the case in all spiritual matters: "All is according to the abundance of the action … As much as one monumental, selfless act can have a great impact on a person and change him or her for the better, 100 smaller deeds will eventually have an even greater influence."[1]

Change is not a one-time occasion; it is a process in which each step is valuable. Once change is initiated, it nourishes itself allowing small changes the potential to snowball into big changes.

---

1. *Rambam, Avos* 3:19. See *Chinuch* Mitzvah 16.

Reuven wants to increase his strength, so he buys a 150-pound weight and plans on lifting it as many times as he can each night. After two repetitions, his muscles ache and he quits. By the third night, he has given up altogether.

Shimon likewise wishes to grow stronger. He buys a 20-pound weight and lifts it 15 times a night for one week. Then he increases to 35 times each night. After that, he buys a 50-pound weight and steadily works his way up. In a matter of months, he is lifting 150 pounds with no strain.

Likewise, each repetition of a small victory over the *yetzer hara* — the *tefillah* you don't skip, the sarcastic remark you don't say — strengthens the *yetzer tov*.[2]

By the same token, small accommodations to the yetzer hara build its power. The battle for our souls is fought choice by choice, mitzvah by mitzvah. God promises that when we choose His will, even in the smallest matter, He will expand the opening we have made in our hearts.

One has to "seize the moment" of Heavenly help to make the "opening the size of the point of a needle," which brings us to complete teshuvah. In fact, the act of grabbing the moment is the person's "opening of the [needle's] point."[3]

---

2. *Sifsei Chaim, Bereishis*, p. 181, s.v. *Beur hadevarim*.
3. From the Alter of Kelm, cited in *Michtav MeEliyahu*, Vol. 4, p. 276, s.v. *V'chasav*.

It is in small steps that we approach God. This is indicated by the three steps forward we take before reciting *Shemoneh Esrei*.[4] They represent the three times[5] the word *Vayigash* — and he approached — appears in *Tanach*.[6] Even though God is everywhere, by deliberately taking three steps forward, we demonstrate our desire to come closer to Him.

> *Each year, the king would venture from the palace to observe his subjects. One year, a poverty-stricken couple was informed that they would be the beneficiaries of a royal visit. The husband immediately began to repaint and repair his rundown dwelling. The wife, however, discouraged his effort. "This is how we live," she said. "Why put on a false face?"*
>
> *"The point," the husband replied, "is to show the king that we are honored by his visit."*

No matter where we stand during the year, it is to our benefit to take small steps to effective teshuvah in anticipation of our King's "visit."

Effective teshuvah mandates knowledge of the relevant halachos. Kindly turn to Laws II: Step One on the Road to Teshuvah (page 208).

---

4. Rav Aharon Leib Shteinman, cited in *Talilei Oros, Parashas Vayigash*, 44:18.
5. (1) *Vayigash Avraham, Bereishis* 18:23; (2) *Vayigash Eilav Yehudah*, ibid. 44:18; (3) *Vayigash Eliyahu, I Melachim* 18:21.
6. *Tanach* is an acronym for *Torah, Neviim, Kesuvim*.

Points to Ponder:

- *It is preferable to consistently do small mitzvos than occasional grand mitzvos.*

- *Setting small goals feeds success and builds into major changes.*

- *Hashem expands the power of our small efforts.*

May today's learning be a zechus
לע"נ Rav Dovid ben Rav Simcha Bunim זצ"ל

Strategy 3: Increase Yiras Shamayim

*I*f service to God is a Jew's "job,"[1] then *yiras Shamayim*[2] is his tool for performing it. A Jew is no more able to live a full Jewish life without *yiras Shamayim*[3] than a carpenter is able to bang in a nail without a hammer. This is the lesson King David taught when he wrote:[4] "Serve God with *yirah* …" "With *yirah*" means that we are to serve God with a "tool" called *yirah*.[5] *Yirah* is the

---

1. *Chofetz Chaim Zechor L'Miriam*, Ch. 5, p. 14; *Chovas HaShemirah*, Ch. 8, *Os* 15.

2. See *Pachad Yitzchak, Shabbos, Maamar* 2, *Os* 2, on the difference between "*yiras Shamayim*" and "*yiras Hashem*." See also *Derech Chaim, Avos* 1:3 for an explanation of why although "*yiras Shamayim*" and "*yiras Hashem*" exists, only "*ahavas Hashem*" exists, but not "*ahavas Shamayim*."

3. See *Chinuch*, Mitzvah 432.

4. *Tehillim* 2:11.

5. *Nefesh HaChaim, Shaar* 4, Ch. 4, cited in *Matnas Chaim, Maamarim* Vol. 2, p. 349,

tool that secures our connection with God,[6] ensuring that we cling to His will with tenacity.[7]

Rabbeinu Yonah[8] explains that of all the qualities one must possess to serve Hashem, *yirah* is first and foremost as the Torah[9] lists *yirah* first: "Hashem, your God, shall you follow and Him shall you fear; His commandments shall you observe and to His voice shall you hearken; Him shall you serve and to Him shall you cleave."

Although the word *yirah* as used in the Torah[10] is translated and understood as "fear"[11] the *Rambam*[12] defines *yirah* as "awe." Recognizing Hashem's greatness not only leads us to love Him, but to be "in awe" of Him as well.[13] However, despite the distinction drawn by *Rambam*, the two definitions of *yirah* are really two levels of the same phenomenon.[14]

---

s.v. *K'var dibarnu.*

6. *Matnas Chaim, Maamarim*, Vol. 2, p. 349, s.v. *K'var dibarnu.* See *Berachos* 6b, which states that the entire world was created only for the sake of the person who fears God.

7. See *Mishnas Rav Aharon*, Vol. 4, p. 111.

8. *Iggeres HaTeshuvah*, cited in *Sifsei Chaim Middos V'Avodas Hashem*, Vol. 2, p. 469.

9. *Devarim* 13:5.

10. *Devarim* 13:5, 10:20; *Koheles* 12:13.

11. Including *Devarim* 10:20, "*Es Hashem Elokecha Tirah* ..." the source in the Torah for the mitzvah of *yirah*.

12. *Hilchos Yesodei HaTorah* 2:2.

13. Ibid. *Rikanti* on Vayeira explains that there is *yiras haromemus*, whose origins are from love, similar to a child whose love for his father is so great that he fears that he may not fulfill the will of his father.

14. *Mesillas Yesharim*, Ch. 24. See *Reishis Chachmah, Shaar HaYirah*, Ch. 1, which

The *yirah* that we define as "fear" is *yiras ha'onesh,* the lesser level of *yirah* that is the fear of Hashem's punishing us for sinning, either in this world or the Next. The greater level of *yirah* — *yiras haromemus,* which is awe of Hashem — is associated with recognizing Hashem's greatness, which inspires us to love Him.[15]

In order to sin, a person pushes away his *yirah.* In order to do teshuvah, he must let this awareness back into his consciousness.[16] Whether a person is driven by *yiras ha'onesh* or *yiras haromemus,* there can be no teshuvah without some aspect of *yirah.*[17]

A person who accepts God as the King over every aspect of Creation, and who believes that his own deeds[18] invoke reward or punishment in both this world and the Next,[19] is driven to look for the meaning in his life's circumstances. In contradistinction, those who believe their misfortunes are the result of coincidences or bad luck have lost their connection to God, the

---

states that there are three levels of *yirah.* See also *Sifsei Chaim, Middos VaAvodas Hashem,* Vol. 2, p. 496 for a full discussion of the three levels of *yirah.* See *Tzidkas HaTzaddik, Siman* 194, where Rav Tzadok HaKohen teaches that there are four levels in *yiras Shamayim.*

15. *Chinuch,* Introduction, s.v. *Aval,* cited by *Be'ur Halachah, Orach Chaim, Siman* 1.
16. See *Be'er Moshe* on Torah, *Bereishis,* Vol. 1, p. 200, s.v. *Bereishis osios* which states that teshuvah itself is bound with *yirah.* The letters in the word *bereishis* (in the beginning) are the same as in *y'rei tasheiv,* with awe, repent. See also *Michtav MeEliyahu,* Vol. 1, p. 240.
17. *Mishnas Rav Aharon,* Vol. 2, p. 151.
18. *Rosh Hashanah* 34b.
19. *Ruach Chaim* 4:3, s.v. *Oh,* cited in *Matnas Chaim,* Vol. 2, p. 33, s.v. *V'yeish l'ha'ir.*

Torah, and mitzvos.[20] A belief in happenstance stops teshuvah in its tracks.[21]

The Torah,[22] itself, decries a belief in happenstance, including it among the sins that evoke tragedies.[23] The *Rambam*[24] warns, "One should not be like agnostics who go with happenstance in their hearts."

Misfortune can only motivate us toward teshuvah if we have *yirah:* the firm, internal knowledge that everything that happens is Hashem's response to our every word and deed. The *Ramban* derives this concept from the verse "Hashem, your God, shall you follow and Him shall you fear."[25] He explains, "One should believe that it is in Hashem's hands to eradicate life and to give life, and He counts sins and compensates with reward." For the person with *yirah,* teshuvah is the clear path to a life of blessing.

Effective teshuvah mandates knowledge of the relevant halachos. Kindly turn to Laws III: That Lingering Odor (page 212).

---

20. See *Matnas Chaim*, Vol. 2, p. 60, s.v. *HaRambam*.

21. *Ohr HaChaim, Vayikra* 26:21

22. ad loc.

23. *"If you behave with happenstance with Me and refuse to heed Me, then I shall lay a further blow upon you."*

24. *Sefer HaMitzvos*, Mitzvah 4.

25. *Devarim* 13:5.

Points to Ponder:

- Yirah is the primary tool for serving God.
- Yirah enables a person to recognize God's hand in the events of his life, thereby motivating teshuvah.

A Father's Message

*I*n Shevat 5694 (January 1934), Rav Dessler was in London, away from his family during the occasion of his son's bar-mitzvah. Rav Dessler wrote the following letter to his son:[1]

I was very happy that you have begun to don tefillin. Thank God, until now you have prepared yourself to perform mitzvos. However, my dear son, you need to know that much, much more preparation is required of you. The essence of all the essential principles of Torah is yiras Shamayim ...

Do you know what yiras Shamayim is and how to prepare yourself for such a broad-based mitzvah? [Do you know that] one who has yiras Shamayim is able to observe the complete Torah? And the one lacking in yiras Shamayim has not prepared himself at all.

---

1. *Michtav MeEliyahu*, Vol. 4, p. 308.

Even if one thinks in his mind that he desires to observe Torah and mitzvos, he knows that practically speaking, when the time comes and he is faced with some desire to the contrary or the Evil Inclination grabs hold of him with whatever reason his heart desires, he will abandon his notion to perform the mitzvah. How, then, will it be possible to prepare himself that he should not abandon the mitzvah he contemplated? Only yiras Shamayim ... will enable him to not turn away from the Torah's path and the mitzvos."

Rav Dessler provides a powerful metaphor explaining the indispensable role of *yiras Shamayim:*

Have you ever seen someone who builds a beautiful house to live in, and neglects to include a door? All his possessions and riches are jeopardized as if he himself discarded them in the street.

Similarly, one who lacks yiras Shamayim is left without protection from difficulties and hurdles, because ... he has nothing in his heart to hold him back. He will invariably be open to the Evil Inclination, which will enter his heart whenever it wants. And he will do all that the Evil Inclination wants him to do. It will result in lawlessness."

Rav Dessler concludes:

Yiras Shamayim and only yiras Shamayim is the "watchman" that can guard all the wealth of Torah and mitzvos with which we deal. And how do we achieve yiras Shamayim? …. We, by ourselves, must build it and have it enter into our hearts[2]…. Whoever is very attentive to the words of mussar will gradually become accustomed to it, and yiras Shamayim will enter into his heart.

Therefore, my precious child, the desire of my soul, pay close attention to what I am telling you. After all, these are the words of your loving father whose hopes all depend on you …

Effective teshuvah mandates knowledge of the relevant halachos. Kindly turn to Laws IV: Never Again (page 215).

Points to Ponder:

- *Yiras Shamayim is the essential underpinning of one's service to God.*

- *Like a house without a door, a Jew without yiras Shamayim is vulnerable to the yetzer hara's theft of his spiritual wealth.*

---

2. Hashem will not give it to us, as the Talmud (*Berachos* 33b) states: "Everything is in Heaven's hands except for fear of Heaven, which is in man's hands."

Constant Blessings

*H*ow do we maintain a constant state of *yiras Shamayim*? Certainly, anyone with eyes, a mind, and a heart can occasionally arrive at a sense of awe by observing the majesty of God's Creation.[1] A stunning sunset can bring tears to your eyes. A newborn baby can fill your heart with wonder. The night sky can overwhelm your senses with its vastness.

But *yiras Shamayim* is not meant to be a momentary revelation; it is one of the six mitzvos[2] in which a Jew is commanded to constantly engage.[3] We are commanded to have *yirah*, which incorporates not only fear of God, but also, constant awareness

---

1. *Michtav MeEliyahu,* Vol. 3, p. 161, s.v. *Derech hisbonanus.* See *Rambam, Hilchos Yesodei HaTorah* 2:2.
2. *Chinuch,* Mitzvah 432.
3. *Chinuch,* Intro. s.v. *Avel,* cited by *Beur Halachah, Orach Chaim, Siman* 1, s.v. *Hu klal baTorah.*

that He is the Creator of all we see.[4] Therefore, the blessings said during the day were formulated.[5]

As the *Rambam*[6] states:

> *Just as one must recite a blessing when deriving pleasure, he must also recite a blessing before doing any mitzvah ... The Sages also established many blessings of praise and thanksgiving and in supplication ... All blessings can be divided into three categories: blessings of pleasure; blessings of mitzvos; and blessings of praise, thanksgiving, and supplication; so that one will be ever cognizant of his Creator and be fearful of Him.*

A day that is saturated with the mindful recitation of blessings is a day infused with *yiras Shamayim.*[7]

Since reciting the blessings is intended to foster *yiras Shamayim,* we begin our day with the morning blessings, *Birchos HaShachar.*[8] By immediately acknowledging the numerous miracles involved in simply waking up alive and functional, we accept upon ourselves the "yoke of Heaven" that can carry us through the day.[9]

---

4. *Rambam, Sefer HaMitzvos,* Mitzvah 4.
5. See *Chovos HaLevavos, Shaar Avodas Elokim,* Ch. 2.
6. *Hilchos Berachos* 1:3.
7. See *Menachos* 43a, regarding reciting 100 *berachos* each day. See also *Orach Chaim, Siman* 46, *Se'if* 3; *Mishneh Berurah,* ibid., *Se'if Katan* 14.
8. See *Shulchan Aruch HaRav, Siman* 46.
9. See *Sifsei Chaim, Middos VaAvodas Hashem,* Vol. 2, p. 478, s.v. *Oda amru; Nefesh Shimshon, Siddur HaTefillah,* p. 45.

In reality, however, these and most other blessings we recite can quickly become rote. As such, they cannot help us to grow in *yiras Shamayim.*

A powerful solution to that problem is to realize that it is only through our blessings[10] and prayers[11] that God's goodness comes into the world. We are not merely reciting words, but actually, activating the supply system of Creation, drawing forth the spiritual power that enables the tree to bear fruit, the ground to yield bread, the eyes to see, the limbs to move, the Jewish people to possess their special closeness to God, and so forth.

By envisioning each of these gifts flowing into our life as we recite the blessing, the words come alive.[12] They become a creative act that brings good into the world, and the individual reciting it builds within himself a constant connection to God and His loving care.

Effective teshuvah mandates knowledge of the relevant halachos. Kindly turn to Laws V: Defining "Never" (page 218).

Points to Ponder:

- *Yiras Shamayim is a constant mitzvah requiring awe of God and awareness of Him as the Creator and Sustainer of everything.*

---

10. *Berachos* 35b.
11. *Bereishis* 2:5 *Rashi,* s.v. *Adam ayin,* Yoma 70b; *Shabbos* 10a, *Rashi,* s.v. *Chayei Olam.*
12. See Day 40, Technique 10: Visualize Success.

- *Reciting blessings is a means to maintain our awareness of God's benevolence.*

- *Reciting a blessing is a real force in bringing God's gifts into one's life.*

May today's learning be a zechus

לע"נ Chaya Reizel bas Yisroel Yosef ע"ה

Dedicated by her son and his family

For Your Protection

*D*espite the uplifting reality of *yirah,* most people do not feel awe all day every day. We understand that *yiras Shamayim* can save us from sin, much like a pain in one's chest can provide the warning that will save a person from a fatal heart attack. We also understand that the stark awareness of God's presence helps us control our words and actions.

Even so, most people find the awareness of such close Divine scrutiny to be uncomfortable. Making it a constant mind-set is therefore even more difficult. Very few people would feel at ease in having their every move monitored by a video camera, even if they behaved in an exemplary fashion. Yet the sense of *yirah* sets up just such a situation, in which we must always have in mind that everything we do and say is seen, recorded, and judged.

On a deeper level, however, there is a feeling of comfort in living one's life in awe of God. A person who continually senses God's awesome presence consistently senses His protection. As King David writes: "*Gam ki eileich b'gei tzalmaves lo irah ra ki Atah imadi*, Though I walk in the valley overshadowed by death, I will fear no evil, for You are with me."[1]

> *Five-year-old Dovid can't wait to ride his new bike up and down the sidewalk in front of his house. It sits in the driveway waiting for him and his little heart is brimming with eagerness to get out there and ride.*
>
> *At the same time, he's scared. The big boy who lives across the street might run over and swipe his new bike out from under him, just as he swiped Dovid's ball, his kite, and his watergun. Worse yet, his other neighbor's frisky little puppy might race out of the yard and chase him. There's another danger too; Dovid knows he has to be very careful to stay on the sidewalk, because if his father sees him riding in the road, he'll lose his bike privileges for a whole week. "Why do parents have to be so strict?" he mumbles to himself.*
>
> *The little boy's desire to ride his bike far outweighs his anxieties and he asks his father permission to go outside.*
>
> *"Go and enjoy your new bike," his father says. "But pay very careful attention to stay on the sidewalk. I will be watch-*

---

1. *Tehillim* 23:4.

ing you and checking on you every few minutes, so don't forget!"

> *Dovid leaves the house happy. His father will be watching. If the puppy chases him or the bully bothers him, his father will protect him. True, he has to stay on the sidewalk rather than riding in the road like the older kids. But even this, he knows, is for his own protection. Being loved, being protected, being watched — it all comes from the same source.*

The heart of this child reflects the comfort and security *yiras Shamayim* confers upon those who are willing to make their Creator the foremost presence in their lives.

Effective teshuvah mandates knowledge of the relevant halachos. Turn to Laws VI: Viduy/Verbal Confession (page 221).

Points to Ponder:

- *Even though yirah is an essential tool of our spiritual lives, the constant awareness of God's presence may be uncomfortable.*

- *With God's constant scrutiny comes His constant protection.*

- *In building yirah, we not only prevent ourselves from sinning, but foster a sense of security in our lives.*

May today's learning be a zechus לע"נ Dovid Levi ben Yitzchok ל"ז
Dedicated by his son and his family

Strategy 4: Make It Real

Two men are walking along the train tracks. When the conductor of an oncoming train notices them, he begins to blast a shrill warning whistle. Both men hear the whistle. One is a simple farmer who has never seen a train. Unaware of what the sound means, he continues walking, enjoying the view and the sound of the whistle. The other person, a city dweller, understands the warning and immediately flees from the oncoming danger.

While both men physically hear the noise of the whistle, only the second one can be said to have properly heard and understood the message: "Leap into action and save your life. Your future is in your hands!"

Are we like the city dweller or the country boy in our response to the "warning whistle" of Elul and the Yamim Noraim? We are a little of each. Like the city dweller, we know what we are hearing. It is Elul, and Rosh Hashanah is speeding toward us. Like the country boy, however, we do not *feel* the urgency to swing into action and do what is necessary to save our lives.

The reason we are able to know and yet not act is because knowledge in our heads does not have the power to move us to action. Only when the knowledge enters our hearts — becomes a reality as certain as a train hurtling down the tracks — do we feel the internal drive to act.

> *This divide between heart and head was the subject of a lecture by Rav Elyah Lopian. He based his words on the verses in the Haftarah read on Shabbos Shuvah, the Shabbos proceeding Yom Kippur:*
>
> *"Return, O Israel, to Hashem, your God"— Return, O Israel, until you say in your mouth and remember, constantly, that Hashem is your God. That means you should know and feel that Hashem is your Caretaker for everything. Why do we not feel this? The end of the verse is the reason —"for you have stumbled through your iniquity."*
>
> *What is the solution? The beginning of the next verse provides the answer — "Take words with you and return to Hashem." Take the words into your heart and return to Hashem. This must be a feeling that resides in one's heart, since knowledge alone does not change behavior. Motivation to change emanates from feeling.*[1]

---

1. *Lev Eliyahu, Maareches HaTeshuvah*, p. 347.

In fact, a deeper reading of *yirah*, the Hebrew word for "awe/fear," discloses that it shares the same root as the word "*re'iyah* — seeing."[2] In the simplest sense, *yirah* means "seeing" the reality of the consequences.

Imagine if we could see the germs left on a drinking glass. No doubt, we would be powerfully motivated to scrub it with soap and hot water to avoid contamination. Without that visual evidence, however, one tends to give the glass a quick rinse and consider it clean enough. Likewise, if we could see the impact of our sins on our souls, we would waste no time finding ways to do teshuvah. However, when we do not "see," then it is more difficult to motivate ourselves to expend the energy on teshuvah.[3]

In our struggle to change, we have to cultivate the emotions necessary to boost our motivation. In that way, we can make something real of our hope to do teshuvah, to change our lives for the better and to merit a year full of blessing and success.

Effective teshuvah mandates knowledge of the relevant halachos. Kindly turn to Laws VII: Laws of Verbal Confession (page 225).

---

2. Rav Tzaddok Hakohen, *Machshevos Charutz*, *Os* 18.

3. Rabbi Shlome Wolbe, *Koveitz Torani, Am HaTorah, Mahadura* 4, *Choveres* 14, 5766, p. 22.

Points to Ponder:

- We know intellectually that teshuvah is necessary, but that knowledge does not easily translate into action.

- Yirah inspires us to see in a concrete way the consequences of our misdeeds.

- The more we make Hashem a reality in our lives, the greater our motivation for teshuvah will be.

"Fire"

In the early years of the Volozhiner Yeshivah, an outstanding student became very ill. Another student accompanied him home. En route, the boys spent a night at an inn. When the innkeeper presented the bill, they were 7 cents short. The ill student took responsibility for the balance. When he arrived home, he gave the other student 7 cents with instructions to pay the innkeeper. Shortly thereafter, the ill student passed away.

Several weeks later, the deceased boy appeared to Rav Chaim Volozhiner in a dream. He reported that he merited entry into Gan Eden; however, his friend had neglected to pay the innkeeper. Until the innkeeper received the 7 cents, the boy would not be allowed into Gan Eden. The deceased was allowed to request from his Rebbe that the bill be paid. Rav Chaim immediately directed the other student to pay the bill, which he did.[1]

---

1. Transmitted by Rav Chaim Volozhiner to R' Zundel of Salant, to R' Yisroel Salanter, to the Alter of Kelm, to his son R' Rabbi Zvi Hirsch Braude, to Rav Elyah

s the story conveys, everything we do in this world has our name on it. Our moral accounts must be balanced to the penny so that there will be no accusations to greet us in the Next World. The realization that every act has real spiritual consequences provides a sturdy counterbalance to the desires that tug at our hearts. *Chovos HaLevavos*[2] explains:

> *Physical pleasures, as opposed to man's intellect, are with him from his youth. His attachment to them is firm and it increases as these pleasures become necessary to him. Therefore … man requires external forces to help him stand firm …*

Concretizing the destructive power of sin helps a person stand fast. In fact, throughout Torah, this approach is used to enable people to internalize that which they cannot fully comprehend.[3] A visual image arms the intellect with ammunition against the passions of the heart, as we see from this story.[4]

> *Rav Amram Chasida once felt himself being overcome by an intense passion to sin. He spaced his feet apart and dug in his heels to resist taking another step. He then shouted, "There is a*

Lopian. Cited in *Inspiration and Insight*, Vol. 1, translated and arranged by Rabbi Shimon Finkelman, ArtScroll/Mesorah, pp. 29-31 and p. 31, fn. 2.

2. *Shaar Avodas Elokim*, Chapter 2.

3. See *Rashi, Shemos* 19:18, s.v. *HaKivshan; HaKuzari, Maamar 3, Os 5; Malbim* on *Mishlei* 12:25.

4. *Kiddushin* 81a.

fire in the house of Amram." When the Sages who ran out to help him found out that there was no fire, they petulantly responded, "You have shamed us."[5]

Why did Rav Amram shout "fire" when there was no fire? To Rav Amram, the "fire" was real.[6] The "fire" of the Evil Inclination was consuming him from within.

The visual image of "fire" has been used by our Sages to describe Gehinnom.[7] They state that fire is one-sixtieth of Gehinnom,[8] a description that enables anyone who has ever felt the singe of a flame to gain some grasp of a concept which is, in reality, indescribable.

By attaching a visual image to the outcome of sin, we can hope to satisfy the advice of *Rabbeinu Yonah*:[9] "Make the words of *yiras Shamayim* fluent on your lips ... Fear God and keep His commandments, for that is man's whole duty."[10]

Effective teshuvah mandates knowledge of the relevant halachos. Kindly turn to Laws VIII: The Final Hurdle (page 229).

---

5. See *Iyun Yaakov*, ad loc.
6. *Maharsha*, ad loc., s.v. *Nura bei Amram*.
7. *Berachos* 57b.
8. See *Michtav MeEliyahu*, Vol. 1, p. 296 that there are other metaphors for Gehinnom.
9. *Sefer HaYirah*, s.v. *Tamid hargel*.
10. *Koheles* 12:13. See *Berachos* 6b.

Points to Ponder:

- Support is necessary to strengthen one's mind to control his heart.

- Knowing that every small act has eternal repercussions provides powerful support to resist urges that might harm someone else or lead to sin.

Lovingly dedicated l'ilui nishmas our mother,
Miriam bas Yisroel Menachem,
by the Racer, Nestlebaum, Shaffren and Benvenisti families.

DAY 25

Strategy 5:
Damage Control

Shmuli accidentally threw a ball through Mr. Stein's window. The glass shattered all over the kitchen table, where several platters of smoked fish waited to be taken into the dining room. There, Mr. Stein's guests were seated, ready to celebrate his 70th birthday. The noise frightened the Steins' daughter, who jerked her hand and spilled her cup of fruit punch on the couch where she was seated. The punch dripped onto the carpeting. Mrs. Stein injured her back trying to scrub the stain.

When Shmuli's father called and offered to pay to replace the windowpane, Mr. Stein's response was, "That doesn't begin to pay for all the damage!"

$\mathcal{I}$f the Steins sued Shmuli's family for the damage done by his ball, it is doubtful whether the judge would be able to calculate the total value of the ruined birthday party, Mrs. Stein's pain, the guests' discomfort on one hand, and Shmuli's embarrassment on the other. God, however, judges with absolute accuracy, calculating every harm arising from a person's misdeed.

The all-encompassing nature of God's judgment is illustrated in the narrative of the world's first murder. After Kayin killed his brother Hevel, God inquired, "What have you done? The sounds of your brother's bloods cry out to Me from the ground."[1] The plural form of the word *"dam"* (blood) indicates that Kayin not only killed his brother, but he also killed his descendants.[2] A person's value is not assessed only according to what he is at the moment; it encompasses the vast potential in each person.

No one can accurately assess the ultimate impact of a sin. Therefore, the spiritually sensitized person sees the potential harm as too great to risk. He strives to avoid any sin and to perform teshuvah to erase any sin he might have committed.

> *When Rabban Yochanan ben Zakkai was on his deathbed, his students came in to visit him. When he saw them, he began to cry: "I have two paths before me: one leading to Gan Eden and one leading to Gehinnom and I do not know on which path they are taking me. Should I not cry?"* [3]

---

1. *Bereshis* 4:10.
2. *Rashi*, ad loc.
3. *Berachos* 28b.

When the saintly Rabban Yochanan saw his students, he became acutely aware of the vast breadth of his potential liability in his dealings with them. Not only the students standing before him, but their children, grandchildren, and great-grandchildren would be affected by mistakes he might have made. Realizing that he would be held accountable for all of this, he became afraid and doubtful as to his place in Gan Eden.[4]

The precision of God's justice is something that is simple to understand;[5] Hashem is truthful. That is what Moshe Rabbeinu meant when he said, "The Rock — perfect is His work, for all His paths are justice."[6] His judgment applies to everyone and He punishes all sins."

This implies that there is no way to escape liability for a sin, and yet a different verse[7] states that God will forgive us. In fact, both are true. Teshuvah is the distinguishing factor, the means God has given us to remake ourselves over and over again, each time closer to His image.

Effective teshuvah mandates knowledge of the relevant halachos. Kindly turn to Laws IX: Reparing Character Flaws (page 233).

---

4. See *Sichos Mussar, Shaarei Chaim, Maamar* 39, p. 164, s.v. *V'Nireh she'chumras ha'onesh* [5732 *Maamar* 3].

5. *Mesillas Yesharim*, Ch. 4, s.v. *V'zeh davar*.

6. *Devarim* 32:4.

7. *Bamidbar* 14:20.

Points to Ponder:

- *God's justice is precise, taking all contingencies and outcomes into consideration.*

- *Teshuvah absolves us of our transgressions, along with any potential effect.*

A Public Service

The Jewish nation were given 613 mitzvos while non-Jews have seven. Yet if a Jew transgresses just one of the 613, he is considered a sinner.

What makes a Jew's relatively minuscule transgression cast so great a shadow on his soul? Consider the impact of a grain of sand blown by the wind. If it lands on your hand, you may not even feel it. If however, it lands in your eye, you are in agony. A hand and an eye are both essential, but they have different strengths and sensitivities. The same applies to a Jew and a non-Jew. While both are Hashem's wondrous creations, they have different strengths and sensitivities to suit their different tasks in the world.[1]

---

1. Lazer Beams: www.lazerbrody.net, *No Easy Way Out*, Rabbi Lazer Brody, September 2, 2008.

To all but the very greatest *tzaddikim*, the impact of a sin in the spiritual world is rarely visible here on earth. Yet it is no less real than the impact of invisible radiation or carbon dioxide let loose in the world. The Chofetz Chaim[2] explains that the detrimental effects begin at the very moment of sinning, as conveyed in the Torah's[3] warning:

> *See, I present before you **today** a blessing and a curse ... And the curse: if you do not listen to the commandments of Hashem, your God, and you stray from the path that I command you today ...*

Hashem has given the Jewish people a sensitive position in a vast, universal operation, trusting us to have faith in His leadership and to do our part to the best of human ability.

> *A 17-year veteran employee in Israel's Dimona nuclear plant was asked if he knew whether Israel has an atom bomb. He answered, "Believe me, I don't have a clue what I am working on. I sit in a cubicle with a window. An object is passed through the window with instructions on what to do with it. It could be for a bomb, it could be for a table. I have no way of knowing."*

Like this worker, who knows only that he is a vital cog in a

---

2. *Shem Olam*, Part 2:9.

3. *Devarim* 11:26-28.

complex system, we know that we are working within Hashem's complex universe. Any deviation from His instructions — our Torah — damages the entire system.[4]

Our deeds affect our individual fates,[5] yet, we are not acting only as individuals. A Jew's actions impact the entire universe.

> *Rav Yisroel Salanter once remarked that time wasted from Torah study in the holy city of Kovno causes Shabbos desecration in the secularized homes of France.*

Teshuvah not only influences the judgment God passes on each of us, but also judgment on the world collectively.[6] Furthermore, all the people who could have prevented our sins are spared their responsibility[7] for our actions when we erase the sin through teshuvah.[8]

In far-greater measure than sin brings troubles to our world, teshuvah brings blessing.[9] Teshuvah leads us to new heights, inspiring our Sages to say, "In the place where *baalei teshuvah* stand, even the completely righteous are not able to stand."[10]

---

4. *Nefesh Shimshon*, Thirteen Principles of Faith, Feldheim Publ., pp. 270-271.
5. *Ani Maamim*, Principle 11.
6. *Kiddushin* 40b; *Rambam, Hilchos Teshuvah* 3:1,2.
7. *Shevuos* 39a.
8. Rama MiFano, cited by *Gilyon HaShas* on *Yoma* 86b and *Yad Yosef; Maharit*, cited by *Tosefes Yom HiKippurim*.
9. *Sanhedrin* 100b; *Sotah* 11a. See also *Rashi, Shemos* 20:6; *Rif* on *Ein Yaakov; Maharsha; Yoma* 86b, s.v. *she'bishvil*.
10. *Berachos* 34b; *Sanhedrin* 99a.

The one who does teshuvah, despite having experienced the "pleasure" of following his impulse, takes hold of himself and breaks away from the sin for the sake of repairing his relationship with Hashem. That is why he is so beloved, and his teshuvah possesses a power that can elevate the worlds.

Effective teshuvah mandates knowledge of the relevant halachos. Kindly turn to Laws X: Middos Make The Man (page 236).

Points to Ponder:

- *Every Jew has a specific, highly sensitive role in Hashem's supervision of the universe.*

- *By transgressing, we damage the functioning of the world.*

- *Teshuvah not only repairs our own situation, but helps to bring a positive judgment to the world.*

Productive Fear

In seventh grade, Yaakov was often disruptive in class, while the other boys were already able to concentrate and learn. His rebbi had tried time and again to inspire him to change his ways. Having exhausted all positive paths, one day, his rebbi took him aside and had a talk with him.

"You know that next year, you'll be applying to high school," the rebbi reminded him. "Who is going to accept you? You're going to end up in a high school for troubled boys, and then you'll have trouble too!"

"It doesn't matter," Yaakov replied despondently. "I can't learn and a kid like me is anyway gonna get into trouble."

The rebbi had hoped that his effort to instill a fear of consequences might rouse Yaakov to action. He had hoped to hear, "I better buckle down and get serious!" Instead, his words triggered nothing but despair.

If a person is suffused with fear of the consequences of his sins, will the inevitability of sin in every human life leave him feeling that effort is futile? Might he not feel that teshuvah cannot succeed, since, inevitably, he will sin again and become liable for all the consequences of his mistake?

The Torah[1] recognizes the paralyzing impact of sin when, referring to Jewish soldiers going to war, it states, "Who is the man who is fearful and fainthearted? Let him go and return to his house." Yet, the motivational value of fear is also recognized, as in the verse,[2] "Fortunate is the man who always fears."[3] The discrepancy is reconciled by identifying the source of the fear. When a person fears separation from Hashem, his fear can motivate him to contemplate his spiritual situation and resolve to improve through teshuvah.[4]

Recognition of the distance we put between ourselves and Hashem when we sin — and the dire consequences of that separation — should indeed sadden us. Yet, the broken heart is the optimal vessel for teshuvah. Until a person feels the piercing pain of "What have I done!" he is not ready to change his ways.

On the other hand, what of the reaction of a person like Yaakov in the opening story? What if fear of sin, instead of inspiring renewed effort, leaves a person feeling depressed and empty?

---

1. *Devarim* 20:8.

2. *Mishlei* 28:14.

3. See *Shaarei Teshuvah* 1:20.

4. *Ohr Yisroel*, Letter 7.

In that case, a person can think, *It doesn't matter what I do. I'm nothing anyway.* This can lead to further sin rather that to teshuvah, which can not only bring troubles upon the person, but upon the world as well, as we discussed in yesterday's lesson.

The resolution is to know that despair and hopelessness are unwarranted; Hashem loves all of us, even the person who is brokenhearted due to his sins. As it is stated,[5] "Hashem is close to the brokenhearted" and, "The sacrifices God desires are a broken spirit."[6]

Knowing that sin has dire consequences is not meant to send a person plunging into a sea of despair, but rather, to spur the regret that in turn inspires teshuvah. It is the teshuvah that blossoms from the fear and regret that brings unlimited blessing into the world. The Talmud[7] states, "Great is repentance for it brings healing to the world," as we find, the blessing in *Shemoneh Esrei* "Heal us, Hashem" comes after the blessing "Forgive us, our Father."[8]

Although sin has a devastating effect on a person's life, teshuvah can truly overturn all these troubles, vastly enhancing our lives. Most important of all, teshuvah imbues our souls with their only source of real joy: a closer, purer relationship with our Father in Heaven.

---

5. *Tehillim* 34:19.
6. Ibid. 51:19.
7. *Yoma* 86a.
8. *Kuntres Eitzos Lizkos B'Din*, p. 45.

Effective teshuvah mandates knowledge of the relevant halachos. Kindly turn to Laws IX: Asking Forgiveness (page 238).

Points to Ponder:

- *When fear stems from regret over the distance between us and Hashem created by our sins, it has a positive impact.*
- *The negative emotion of fear gives rise to the positive power of teshuvah, which can overturn all the troubles brought about by sin and bring blessing in far greater measure.*

May today's learning be a zechus for
Yitzchok Ze'ev ben Brocha Bruria
לברכה והצלחה in all his endeavors

Strategy 6: Study Mussar, Spiritual Ethics

"I know I should exercise, but I simply don't have time," the patient told his doctor.

"Your blood pressure is creeping up to a dangerous level. If you don't begin exercising, you're risking a heart attack or stroke," the doctor explained.

The next day, the man found a gym near his office and began to spend his lunch-hour exercising. He had suddenly found the time.

Like the patient, most of us have a vague idea of what we must do to promote spiritual health. We know we could do better — learn more Torah, pray with more concentration, give more charity, and so forth — but we don't see real improvement as absolutely necessary.

Mussar enables us to identify which part of our spiritual anatomy is weak, how to repair the damage, and the consequences of failing to respond. Once we comprehend the stark necessity of teshuvah, we can find the few extra minutes to say a blessing correctly or to pray with deep concentration, or add extra learning to our schedule.

In the allegory above, the doctor issues his warning once and the patient institutes a change. Most likely, however, his determination will fade and he will revert to his old habits. But what if he had to visit his doctor every day and report on his progress? No doubt, he would adhere to his program with far more seriousness. *Mussar* is analogous to this daily visit. It not only awakens a person to the need for teshuvah, but reinvigorates his commitment each day it is studied.[1]

It would seem that even without opening a *mussar sefer*, a person could sense that things are not quite right with his life. Nevertheless, there is a wide gap between that feeling and deep-seated motivation to change.

Mussar is the most reliable means for one to overcome the obstacles, diversions, and delusions. That is why Rav Yisroel Salanter[2] writes that teshuvah is not possible without studying *mussar*.[3] *Mussar* is far more than a mere accessory to Torah learning. It is an absolute essential: "Hold fast to moral

---

1. *Sifsei Chaim, Moadim*, Vol. 1, p. 60.

2. *Ohr Yisroel, Iggeres* 14.

3. See *Maarachos HaTeshuvah* (back of *Lev Eliyahu*, Vol. 3), p. 397, s.v. *Kosav*.

instruction, do not let her go; preserve her, for she is your life."[4]

First, one must learn the mitzvos and their halachos, so that he understands what God requires of him.[5] When a person understands the destruction that he causes even with small, private wrongdoings, he builds a firm commitment to follow the right path. Halachah teaches us what to do. *Mussar* inspires us to implement the mitzvos.[6]

Mussar protects against sin in yet another way: by nurturing positive character traits.[7] The main point of studying *mussar* is to avoid duplicity and guile.

No one is beyond the reach of *mussar*.[8] Indeed, renowned Torah leaders count *mussar* as an indispensable part of their learning and life.[9] As one commented, "Believe me! On a day when I do not study *mussar*, I feel that my fear of God is weakened noticeably."[10] In fact, the Chofetz Chaim related that the

---

4. *Mishlei* 4:13.

5. *Rabbeinu Yonah, Shaarei Teshuvah, Shaar* 3, *Os* 3.

6. *Alei Shur*, Vol. 1, p. 87, s.v. *Kach hahalachah*; See ibid. Vol. 1, p. 236.

7. *Mesillas Yesharim*, Ch. 12, s.v. *V'chein b'inyan.*

8. See *Ohr Yisroel*, Letter 3.

9. See *Lev Eliyahu, Parashas Pekudei,* p. 242, s.v. *V'hu mah,* where Rav Elyah Lopian explains that one should not mistakenly think that *mussar* is extra and only for "saintlihood" and without it one can live; it's just not so. Without *mussar* one has no life.

10. Chasam Sofer, *Eitzos LeDinah* pp.28-29. See *Minhagei Chasam Sofer*, Ch. 2, *Os* 4, which states that the Chasam Sofer would teach *mussar* for 15 minutes prior to his daily *shiur* to his students. See *Alei Shur*, Vol. 1, p. 91, s.v. *Ein l'sha'eir,* which states that Rav Naftali Amsterdam wrote in his will, "Every day that I learn *mussar*, all my actions, speech, and thought are much better."

rabbanim who initially opposed the early *mussar* movement [late-19th century] eventually came to the realization that without it, "we have no assurance that our Torah knowledge or our fear of God will be sustained."[11]

Effective teshuvah mandates knowledge of the relevant halachos. Kindly turn to Laws XII: Asking Forgiveness: The Laws (page 242).

Points to Ponder:

- *Studying mussar inspires a person to do teshuvah.*
- *Without mussar, one would not know what needs correcting, nor understand the necessity of correcting it.*

---

11. See *Mishnah Berurah*, *Siman* 1, *Shaar HaTziyun*, *Os* 26. See *Michtav Me'Eliyahu*, Vol. 1, p. 57, s.v. *Aich yavo.*

Effective Mussar

> *"Take it, it's good for you," the mother said as she held a spoon-ful of unpleasant-smelling medication to her child's lips.*
>
> *He refused the remedy. The mother tried to pry his mouth open, but then she had a better idea. She mixed the medicine into a bowl of ice cream. The child gobbled down the treat.*

For many people, the idea of learning *mussar* is like taking unpleasant medicine. They may even believe that the worse it tastes, the better it is for them. Yet, this perspective comes from a lack of understanding as to how to effectively study *mussar*.[1]

Mussar is a form of study that must reach our hearts in order to have an impact.[2] "The knowledge of the brain and the knowl-

---

1. See *Michtav MeEliyahu*, Vol. 1, p. 259, s.v. *Mah naaseh*.
2. See ibid., Vol. 5, p. 423, s.v. *L'kinyan b'lev.* See also ibid., p. 49, s.v. *yeish sh'miah,* which states that *mussar* is most effective with "painting vivid pictures" in one's mind that will enable the message to connect with the person's heart.

edge of the heart are like two different people: one knows what the other does not."[3]

To stir the heart, learning *mussar* with a melody is effective, since music is a language the heart readily understands.[4] Many people have witnessed or experienced the power with which a melody touches one's emotions.

> *Rav Elyah Lopian would learn mussar in a loud voice, using a tune that would capture the heart.[5] Once he gave a mussar discourse in Beis Medrash Govoha of Lakewood. Afterward, several students asked him how to learn mussar. He responded, once again using a full, melodious voice to deliver the powerful emotional content of the words.[6]*

Like medicine, *mussar* is most effective when it is "taken" on a regular schedule. Rav Chaim Ozer Grodzensky made a written commitment to "Study a *mussar sefer* every day."[7]

"One must set a time to learn *mussar* each and every day, be it a small or large amount of time," says the Chofetz Chaim.[8]

3. Rav Simcha Zissel Ziv, cited in *Matnas Chelko* on *Shaarei Teshuvah*, p. 21; *Sifsei Chaim, Middos Va'Avodas Hashem*, Vol. 2, p. 549; *Maaracha HaTeshuvah* (back of *Lev Eliyahu*, Vol. 3), p. 399, s.v. *V'yeish al ha'adam*.

4. *Ohr Yisroel*, Letter 5. See *Lev Eliyahu, Parashas Vayeitzei*, p. 116, s.v. *Od yeish ladaas*.

5. *Lev Eliyahu, Mitoldosov*, p. 41, s.v. *Limud hamussar*.

6. Ibid., p. 42, s.v. *Yadua*.

7. *Rav Pam on the Festivals*, Rabbi Sholom Smith, ArtScroll/Mesorah, p. 42.

8. *Mishnah Berurah, Siman* 1, *se'if katan* 12; ibid., *Siman* 603, *se'if katan* 2.

The optimal way to ensure that the learning leads to action is to learn in a group setting.[9]

Like Torah, *mussar* needs to be learned on a consistent basis. The greatest benefit from studying *mussar* comes from review and repetition, because that helps us to recall concepts we have already learned and have forgotten.[10] As people often have stated after listening to a powerful speech, "It was nothing I haven't heard before, but I needed to hear it again."[11]

Yet, there are many people to whom the word "*mussar*" has negative connotations of self-righteous haranguing or pie-in-the-sky idealism.[12] The most effective *mussar* for this type of person is a vivid, realistic parable that breaks through the resistance and opens up the heart.

> *Rav Chaim Shmulevitz once approached two study partners who asked, "If the study of mussar is so important, why do we study Gemara for hours a day, and mussar for only 20 minutes during the same day?" He responded, "The study of mussar may be likened to the Kodesh HaKodashim of the Holy Temple. The*

9. *Michtav MeEliyahu*, Vol. 5, p. 64, 512.

10. *Mesillas Yesharim*, Introduction, s.v. *Aval hato'eles*. See *Michtav Me'Eliyahu*, Vol. 1, p. 260, s.v. *V'kasav ode.*

11. See *Kuntras Shaarei Ohr*, cited in *Alei Shur*, Vol. 1, p. 88, s.v. *Yesod hachinuch*, where Rav Itzele Peterburger advises that *mussar* is not limited to hearing speeches and reading articles or dissertations. Rather, it must be studied daily, similar to Torah study, which involves deliberation and constant review.

12. *Michtav MeEliyahu*, Vol. 1, p. 259, s.v. *Mah naaseh.*

Kohen Gadol need only enter for a few moments for it to have a very lasting impact upon him."

So, too, if we study Mesillas Yesharim, or Orchos Tzaddikim, or Shaarei Teshuvah, or similar classic works for only a few minutes a day, it will leave an indelible impact upon us, and lead us to new heights![13]

Mussar comes in many forms: speeches, articles, classic, and contemporary *sefarim*.[14] Each suits a specific person. Two classic *mussar sefarim* are *Shaarei Teshuvah* — The Gates of Repentance[15] and *Mesillas Yesharim* — The Path of the Just.[16] Rav Chaim Volozhin once commented that *Shaarei Teshuvah* is appropriate for every Jewish soul for all eras.[17] The Chofetz Chaim said, "Every person, no matter what his nature, can benefit from studying *Mesillas Yesharim*." [18]

---

13. "Hakhel Daily Bulletin," Sivan 1, 5771; June 3, 2011.

14. See *Alei Shur*, Vol. 1, p. 87, s.v. *Es yesodoseha*. Rabbi Yisroel Salanter, founder of the *mussar* movement, established the practicality of studying *mussar*.

15. Rabbeinu Yonah.

16. R' Moshe Chaim Luzzatto, the Ramchal.

17. *Shaarei Teshuvah* is comprised of four "gates." The first gate presents us with Rabbeinu Yonah's 20 stages of teshuvah. The second gate focuses upon the six instances in which we are likely to be inspired to do teshuvah. The third gate offers us ten categories of mitzvos to understand well in order to serve God deeply and knowledgeably. And the fourth gate discusses the idea of Divine "atonement" or ultimate forgiveness.

18. Other renowned *mussar sefarim* are, *Rabbeinu Bachya Ibn Pekudah's Chovos HaLevavos* — The Duties of the Heart — and *Rambam's Shemoneh Perakim* — Eight Chapters.

The Vilna Gaon was once asked to recommend the "best mussar sefer." The Gaon responded, "They are all worthwhile. For me, the best of all is right there on that wall." The disciple glanced at the bookshelves, but he could not locate even one mussar sefer. "My son, you misunderstood," said the Gaon. "When I said that my favorite mussar sefer was on the wall, I meant the clock. Every second of the day, that clock ticks away, reminding me that time is still fleeting.

Points to Ponder:

- *Mussar must be learned in a way that stirs the heart.*
- *A moving melody is an effective way to learn mussar.*
- *Mussar should be learned daily, at a set time, just as Torah is learned.*

May today's learning be a zechus for
Elisheva Deena bas Brocha Bruria
לברכה והצלחה in all her endeavors

Strategy 7:
Focus on the Negative

Eli was his own best friend. He forgave every mistake he made. He believed his own myriad excuses for his failures, lapses, and impulsive actions. He believed in his own innate goodness; if only the world would cooperate, he knew he would be a far better, more productive person. But what could he do? He was surrounded by difficult people and extenuating circumstances. He did the best he could, he told himself, and that was all that could be expected.

*M*ost people are similarly generous in their self-judgment, offering themselves ample excuses for their misdeeds. The person who is capable of cutting though his justifications, reaching into his own heart and objectively assessing what he finds there, has ascended to a level of personal greatness. "I have sinned" may be the three most difficult words to state with complete sincerity.[1]

To some extent, most of us content ourselves with excuses and rationalizations. If we are able to predict them and recognize them when they occur, like warning signs along the road, teshuvah can begin.

The way to break through our self-justifications and find the roots of our spiritual challenges is to focus on the negative. In other words, to list all the faulty reasoning that keeps us from teshuvah, and then, to challenge each one with the unvarnished reality of the situation. In the next few days, we will address the thoughts that take up space in our minds, and learn how to discard them to make room for a powerful new reality.

Rationale: Teshuvah requires an unhealthy focus on guilt and shame. This is unnecessary for me, for "I am basically a good Jew."

Reality: Teshuvah is like a medical imaging test designed to expose dangerous health conditions. A person might prefer to think of himself as healthy, but avoiding the test will lead him in the opposite direction. He has to recognize his problem before he can cure it.

Rationale: To err is human. If God expected perfection, He would have made me perfect.

---

1. ArtScroll's *Yom Kippur Machzor.*

Reality: The *Rambam*[2] utterly rejects such moral avoidance. "Free will is bestowed on every human being … there is no one who can prevent him from doing that which is good or that which is evil." Being "only" human is not a viable excuse for mistakes. Rather, the opposite is true; being human means we are capable of, and therefore responsible for, making the right moral choice.

The Torah[3] urges us to realize that teshuvah is "in your mouth … to perform." The teshuvah process begins "in your mouth," by confessing and thereby accepting responsibility for having sinned. That is where the new era — both for ourselves personally, and for the world — begins.

Points to Ponder:

- *One cannot begin to correct what is wrong, until he looks at himself honestly.*

- *Every rationale used to justify wrongdoing has an opposing reality.*

- *By recognizing these realities, we can clear the path to teshuvah.*

---

2. *Hilchos Teshuvah* 5:1.
3. *Devarim* 30:11,14.

Strategy 8: Accept Responsibility: Who, Me?

*R*ationale: I can't help it. I was born with this trait … I was brought up this way … It's the culture around me … It's my neighborhood … It's my family … It's my job … It's my genes.[1]

Reality: If we transgress one of Hashem's commandments, our first reaction should be one of remorse, combined with an effort to remedy the damage and avoid repeating the sin. But it is impossible to have remorse for something unless we feel responsible for it. If a person believes that circumstances "forced" his actions, he is actually blaming Hashem,[2] Who creates all circumstances, rather than himself, the one who committed the sin.

---

1. *Sefer Yaaros D'vash* Vol. 2, *Drush* 10.
2. See *Sforno, Bereishis* 3:12.

A person who blames others relinquishes the power he has to determine the course of his own life. He allows himself to become a slave of circumstance, blown wherever the wind will carry him. However, a person who accepts personal responsibility recognizes the power of choice that God put into his hands, and makes an effort to build a good life utilizing that power. Accepting personal responsibility includes:[3]

- Acknowledging that you are solely responsible for the choices in your life.
- Accepting the fact that you choose your feelings and thoughts.
- Accepting that you choose the direction for your life.
- Realizing that you cannot blame others for the choices you have made.
- Realizing that you have the power to determine your reaction to any events or actions directed at you, no matter how negative they seem.
- Refusing to indulge in self-pity, but rather, taking charge of your life and giving it direction and reason.
- Internalizing that God equips each person to perfection. If He did not equip you with a certain asset or

3. Adapted from Tools for Personal Growth by James J. Messina, Ph.D., Assistant Professor, Department of Counseling and Psychology at Troy University.

trait, then that trait cannot help you achieve your potential.

- Taking an honest inventory of your strengths, abilities, talents, virtues, and positive points.
- Developing positive, self-affirming, self-talk scripts to enhance your personal development and growth.
- Letting go of blame and anger toward people in your past; realizing that they did the best they could, given the limitations of their knowledge, background, and awareness.

When a person takes these points to heart, he has prepared his mind to embark on teshuvah. The next step is to determine what specific area of his life he is ready to tackle. He can now experience the exhilaration of knowing that some stubborn problem, previously blamed on circumstance, is *not* beyond his ability to improve. Like a person setting out on a mountain hike, one can predict that the road ahead will be daunting, but the view from the top will be worth the climb!

Points to Ponder:

- *One tends to reject personal responsibility for wrongs committed or troubles that beset him.*

- *Without taking responsibility for one's actions, the remorse that leads to teshuvah and change cannot arise.*

- *All aspects of accepting personal responsibility are rooted in our God-given power of free will.*

NOTE:

There is a strong tradition[1] of doing something extra during the days from Rosh Hashanah through Yom Kippur to demonstrate to Hashem that we recognize and seek His nearness and His approval. For example, if one was accustomed to study one folio of Talmud, he should study two folios. If one chapter was his daily limit, he should study two.[2]

In this vein, we will provide two thoughts in the ensuing days through Yom Kippur: "going the extra mile".

Is this putting on a "false face" for Hashem? On the contrary, it is our way of confirming in our own hearts that the King is near to us, the essential first step to effective teshuvah.

---

1. *Orach Chaim*, 683:1. See *Sifsei Chaim*, *Moadim*, Vol. 1, p. 61.
2. *Ashrei HaIsh*, p. 128. See *Vayikra Rabbah*, beginning of Ch. 25.

לע"נ ר' חיים ברוך בן בנימין ז"ל
לע"נ שמואל בן שמעון ז"ל

from their loving grandchildren
Carolyn, Barry, Rachel, Noam & Binyamin Stein

Go With the Flow

*R*ationale: "Everyone in my community does it. How could it be so terrible if all these respectable people do it too?"

Reality: Countering this line of thought, the Torah[1] warns, "Do not go after the majority to do evil." From this verse, *Rabbeinu Bachya* draws the following vital lesson:[2]

> *The plain meaning of this verse is that if you see many people doing something wrong, you should not follow their example. When many people do something wrong, it is easier for a person to think, "So many people are doing this, it can't be so wrong if I do it also." Conversely, the Torah teaches that each person is responsible for his own behavior.*

---

1. *Shemos* 23:2.

2. Cited by Rabbi Zelig Pliskin, *Growth Through Torah*, pp. 195-6.

It takes much strength of character to be different from others for [the sake of] one's ideals. However, anyone who appreciates that the most important thing in the world is to do the will of the Almighty will weigh his own behavior against the Torah standards and not the standards of others, regardless of how numerous they are.

Rationale: Once a person has exhausted his list of people and circumstances to blame for his faults, he might look to himself. But here, too, he can erect an obstacle to undertaking teshuvah — "I'm too far gone to change!"

Reality: *Rabbeinu Yonah* explains that the power of teshuvah is boundless: "Even if they have offended and rebelled exceedingly, and been utterly faithless, He has not closed the doors of repentance to them..."[3]

The Torah informs us that as long as we live, we can do teshuvah. As the *Rambam*[4] paraphrases, "Even if he transgressed throughout his life but repented on the day of his death and died as a penitent, all his sins are forgiven." Even a lifelong sinner can, and therefore must, repent.

In *Yad HaChazakah,*[5] the laws of teshuvah directly follow the laws related to the cardinal sin of idol worship. This sequence

---

3. *Shaarei Teshuvah, Shaar* 1, s.v. *Min hatovos,* citing *Yeshayah* 31:6 and *Yirmiyah* 3:22. See *She'eilos U'Teshuvos, Teshuvos V'Hanhagos*, Vol. 4, *Siman* 148, p. 136, s.v. *Taanos hayetzer hara.*

4. *Hilchos Teshuvah* 2:1.

5. Found at the end of *Sefer HaMada.*

teaches us that there is no sinner, nor any sin, which is beyond teshuvah.[6]

The sense of hopelessness and futility arises from within ourselves. Often, a stumbling block familiar to dieters comes into play. The dieter loses his self-control for a few moments and grabs an extra portion. Rather than pulling himself back on track, he thinks, *Well, that kills the diet for today. I might as well eat whatever I want now.* From that reasoning, he turns a few hundred extra calories into a day devoid of all self-control.

Likewise, the person seeking to deal with an entrenched sin will usually suffer some cracks in his resolve. If he says to himself, *That's that. There's no use going forward with teshuvah. Nothing is going to change,* then his setback turns into a full-fledged defeat. Had he kept moving forward, the setback would have soon faded into the background.

When we embark on teshuvah and at times, disappointingly find ourselves back where we started, we can find strength in the image of the ladder our forefather Yaakov saw in his dream. It was "a ladder stationed on the ground with its head (the top rung) reaching the heavens," and it represented Yaakov's life's task of rung-by-rung spiritual elevation.[7]

A ladder can be used to go in either direction. If we should happen to step down, we must realize that we are still on the

---

6. Manchester Rosh Yeshivah, *Inspiration and Insight*, Vol. 1, translated and arranged by Rabbi Shimon Finkelman, ArtScroll/Mesorah p. 151.
7. *Bereishis* 28:12.

ladder. We have not been thrown to the ground. In fact, it may be that very downward motion that propels us upward, to heights that we never before attained.

No Big Deal

Rationale: Zev picked out a unique, expensive tie in the local men's clothing store. As he approached the check-out counter, he noticed a rack with a nicer tie at a lower price. Instead of returning the first tie to its rack, he placed it on top of some sweaters. "No big deal," he thought, vaguely aware that a potential buyer might not notice the tie, and the owner thereby lose a sale.

*R*eality: Many of the misdeeds a person confesses on Yom Kippur would seem to fit into the category of "no big deal." Nevertheless, their inclusion on the list of sins for which we confess and pound our hearts in contrition means that they are acts for which God requires us to repent.

The Talmud[8] drives home the significance of "insignificant sins" by reminding us that a person who derives just a *perutah*'s (nominal) worth of benefit from consecrated property must atone by bringing an offering worth two *shekels*, which is cal-

---

8. *Kiddushin* 12a, See *Rashi*, ibid., s.v. *Yoseir.*

culated to equal 1,536 *perutos*. This shows that even a small transgression requires a large atonement.[9]

But why is the accounting so strict? *Rabbeinu Yonah* provides the reason.[10] He warns that a person should not focus on the "insignificance" of the sin, but rather, the significance of the One Who has commanded the transgressed mitzvah.

In effect, it is as if God has asked, "Do this small thing for Me," and a person refuses.

> *If the king commands one of his subjects to fight a lion and the subject refuses ... it is not because he is rebelling. Rather, he is afraid of doing battle with the lion. However, if the king orders the subject to close the door and he refuses, then it is clear that he is rebelling against the king and is deserving of severe punishment.*

An additional reason to focus on minor sins is because by capitulating to our *yetzer hara* in these matters, we embolden it. A person essentially appeases the little tyrant within himself, providing him with the arms he needs to become a supreme dictator. As the Talmud[11] warns, "Today the Evil Inclination tells him to commit a 'minor' infraction. Tomorrow he will cajole him into transgressing a more significant sin."

---

9. See *Orach Chaim, Siman* 656, *Se'if* 1 where *Rama* rules that one is obligated to give up all his riches rather than transgress a single negative prohibition.
10. *Shaarei Teshuvah, Shaar* 1, *Os* 38.
11. *Shabbos* 105b.

Finally, if we accept minor sins as an inevitable part of our life — something that does not warrant teshuvah — we do ourselves a great disservice. That is because every sin stands in the way of our connection with Hashem, and the more ingrained a sin becomes, the more difficult it becomes to abandon. If we do not deal with a deficiency when it is small and more easily quashed, we enable it to become a deeply rooted bad habit.

> A salesman was interviewed for a new job. The company offered him a good salary, but it was $2,000 less than he had requested. The salesman thought, "If they are letting such a small amount become an issue, they don't really want me." The company president thought, "If he's letting such a small amount become an issue, he doesn't really want the job."

Likewise, we rationalize that if God is "really" on our side, He won't let our small sins get in the way of our relationship. From Heaven's viewpoint, however, the situation is just the opposite. If we really want to be close to God, how can we allow small sins to get in the way?

Points to Ponder

- *One must judge the righteousness of his actions by Torah standards, not those of society.*
- *It is never futile to undertake teshuvah, no matter what the sin or how long one's history of sin may be.*

- *To overcome setbacks, one must keep moving forward.*

- *Committing small sins emboldens the yetzer hara.*

- *Allowing small sins to become ingrained in our behavior installs a permanent barrier between us and Hashem.*

Strategy 9: Pray

On Rosh Chodesh Elul 5695 (1935), a few short years before the annihilation of European Jewry began in earnest, Rav Dessler wrote the following advice to his son:

> *My dear son, please remember what is before you, the Day of Judgment, which requires great preparation. You must daven from the depths of the heart to arouse Rachmei Shamayim (Mercy from Heaven) that we merit Heavenly Assistance, and that Hashem gives us success in attaining teshuvah from the depths of the heart, for this is the ikar (essence) through which we can emerge innocent in justice, B'ezras Hashem.[1]*

The Talmud teaches[2] that spirituality is the one area of life that Hashem has turned over to Man's control: "Everything is

---

1. *Michtav MeEliyahu*, Vol. 4, p. 313.
2. *Berachos 33b.* See *Rashi,* ibid., s.v. *Hakol b'yedei,* which states that whether a

in the hands of Heaven except *yiras Shamayim*." How, then, can we pray for Hashem to enable us to come closer through teshuvah? How are we able to ask Hashem in the Yamim Noraim *Shemoneh Esrei,* "And so, too, O Hashem, our God, instill Your awe upon all Your works, and Your dread upon all that You have created?" It would seem that we are asking Hashem to impose His will in the one area that He has left to *our* will.

While we cannot ask Hashem to *make* us do the right thing, we can ask Him to help us see ourselves clearly and to awaken our hearts to teshuvah. Since teshuvah is an internal process, we have to work on it from the inside out, starting with our hearts. Prayer, which originates in the heart, is therefore an ideal tool for elevation.[3]

When we pray to Hashem for help in doing teshuvah, we demonstrate that being close to Him and doing His will are our priorities. That is the feeling we express when we recite the fifth blessing of *Shemoneh Esrei,*[4] *"V'hachazireinu b'teshuvah sheleimah l'fanecha"* — influence us to return in complete repentance.

Because *tefillah* and teshuvah are driven by the desire of coming closer to Hashem, when we pray for forgiveness and Divine assistance, we are indeed considered to be doing teshuvah.[5] These prayers are contained in *Shemoneh Esrei*: *"Selach*

---

person will be wicked or righteous is given to man and is not in Heaven's hands.

3. *Sefer HaZikaron L'Baal Michtav MeEliyahu,* Vol. 1, p. 33, s.v. (8) *Ein lanu eitzah.*

4. *"Bring us back, our Father, to your Torah, and bring us near, our King, to Your service, and influence us to return in perfect repentance before You."*

5. *Pachad Yitzchak, Yom HaKippurim, Maamar* 1:2. See ibid., *Maamar* 3:16-17;

lanu" requests forgiveness and *"Hashiveinu"* asks for the ability to repent.

Besides its power to open our hearts to teshuvah, prayer enables our efforts to bear long-lasting results. We can stay on track by asking Hashem to keep difficult challenges and temptations out of our path. Since life is a continual confrontation with temptation, we can and indeed *should* pray for spirituality at all times.[6]

Rav Chaim Volozhin taught his students that prayer could protect them from encountering such challenges as anger,[7] *lashon hara*, looking at improper sights, and other sins that cross one's path uninvited.[8] He advised:

> *Pray before there is a misfortune, because the yiras Shamayim that brings one to pray is what will save [the person] from the test … The [fact that man prays to be saved] declares to his Creator that he recognizes very well the greatness of the [spiritual] test.[9]*

Shaarei Teshuvah 1:41-42.

6. *Maharsha Kiddushin* 81b, s.v, *Harachaman; Shabbos* 156b, s.v. *Uba'ei rachmei; Moed Katan* 28a, s.v. *B'mazala* and *Berachos* 10a, s.v. *Chata'im k'siv.*

7. See *She'al Avicha V'Yagedcha*, Vol. 3, p. 116, which states that a student in Radin once saw the Chofetz Chaim open the doors to the Ark and begin to cry, "Ribbono shel Olam, I admit before you that You created me a Kohen and a Kohen gets angry easily [*Kiddushin* 70a]. Please help me that I should overcome my anger."

8. See *Chayei Olam,* p. 41.

9. Cited in *Matnas Chaim, Maamarim* 2, p. 9; ibid. pp. 197, 303.

We are not alone in our quest to purify our hearts and bring ourselves closer to Hashem. We can turn to God openly, passionately, in our own language and ask Him to free us from our self-imposed bonds. We can share our anguish with Him regarding our trials and failures at self-improvement and by doing so, we acknowledge that only Hashem, in His infinite love, can help us.

Strategy 10: ASAP: The Future Is Now

When a task perceived to be difficult lies ahead, the common human response is to procrastinate. "I'll start tomorrow, when I'm refreshed." "I'll pay next month, when I have more money." "I'll do better when the children get older and I have more peace and quiet."

Concerning teshuvah, the Chofetz Chaim[10] paints a clear picture of the error in this strategy with the following allegory about a servant who has fled from his master:

> *The servant meets a man who advises him to return of his own accord, show remorse for leaving, and promise to serve his*

10. *Zechor L'Miriam*, Ch. 4, pp.13-14.

master faithfully from then on. With that approach, the man
guarantees that the master will forgive him. If, instead, he waits
to be found and brought back against his will, he will no doubt
have to fully account for his decision to flee from his obligations.

Postponing teshuvah has many negative ramifications.[11] By delaying our effort to change, we leave ourselves in a situation of repeating the sin,[12] which begins to seem less and less like a sin,[13] and more like a permissible option.[14] At that point, we might completely lose the impetus to do teshuvah.[15]

How does the impermissible become permissible?[16] It ceases to arouse guilt. If we no longer feel that we are doing wrong, we no longer feel the need to apologize or change.

At Congregation Kol Peh, chazaras hashatz was considered the
perfect time for the men to catch up on one another's news.
When Boruch first moved into the community, he tried not to
become involved in the talk, but he soon realized that his new
neighbors considered him "holier than thou." The first time he
spoke during chazaras hashatz, he felt a burning guilt. But by

---

11. See *Michtav MeEliyahu*, Vol. 1, p. 313, s.v. *Hashem Yisbarach; Tzidkas HaTzaddik, Os* 61. *Mesillas Yesharim*, Ch. 7.

12. *Rabbeinu Yonah, Shaarei Teshuvah, Shaar* 1:2, s.v. *V'da*. See *Koheles Rabbah* 7:15.

13. *Kiddushin* 40a.

14. *Shaarei Teshuvah, Shaar* 1:5, s.v. *Hasheinis*; ibid., *Shaar* 1:2 s.v. *V'da*.

15. *Shaarei Teshuvah* 1:5. See *Matnas Chelko, Sha'arei Teshuvah*, p. 15.

16. *Michtav MeEliyahu*, Vol. 1, p. 122, s.v. *Bechinah* 3.

the end of the first month of partaking in the chatter, he was
initiating conversations himself. He had inured himself to a sin
described in the Shulchan Aruch[17]:

"One should refrain from speaking during the time the
chazan repeats Shemoneh Esrei. And if one spoke, it is a sin."

The period of Elul through Yom Kippur is especially equipped
for teshuvah to succeed.[18] Nevertheless, the optimal time to do
teshuvah is immediately after having sinned.

In any case, when we view our efforts to do teshuvah as solid-
ifying our relationship with Hashem, our resolve to do teshuvah
is most effective.

A newlywed husband sits down to a dinner his young wife has
prepared. He takes a bite of chicken coated in an unusual sauce,
and says, "Hmmm, this is kind of interesting."

Immediately, his wife's smile collapses and her eyes seem
a little moist. "Oh, no! I've insulted her!" the man thinks. On the
spot, he looks her in the eye and says, "That was a foolish thing
for me to say. This is delicious. That's what I meant … I just
never ate it before."

When a person's heart is devoted to another, he responds
instantaneously to anything he thinks might cloud the relationship. By hastening to do teshuvah immediately after a sin, we

---

17. *Siman* 124, *Se'if 7.* "And the sin is too great to bear."
18. *Matnas Chelko* on *Shaarei Teshuvah* p.11.

show God that we are His devoted, beloved people, and that we cannot endure — even for a moment — any distance between us.

Points to Ponder:

- *Tefillah and teshuvah are both driven by the desire to come close to God.*

- *When we pray for forgiveness and Divine assistance, we are considered to be doing teshuvah.*

- *When a person delays teshuvah, he repeats his misdeeds, which then seem permissible to him.*

- *Once a misdeed seems permissible, it no longer stirs the guilt that motivates teshuvah.*

- *Doing teshuvah immediately shows God that we cannot endure, even for a moment, a breach between Him and us.*

By Cory and Jonathan Glaubach in honor of their children,
בתיה פסיה, אברהם לייב, רחל דבורה

CHAPTER
FIVE

Techniques
to an Enduring
Teshuvah

Planning for Victory

*P*erfection is not a human trait. As King Solomon stated, "There is no man in the world who is a *tzaddik* who does only good and does not sin."[1] If a person seeks guidance and correctly analyzes his misdeed, that misdeed becomes a springboard for growth. If he hastily pastes a Band-Aid over the sin, it will only show its face again, perhaps in an even uglier fashion.

Life is a war against the *yetzer hara, a*s King Solomon advises "With strategies he makes war."[2] In this war, above all others, success can come only with a thought-out plan of action. The enduring effect of teshuvah lies not in the depth of our regret or the strength of our commitment to abandon a sin, but in our

---

1. *Koheles* 7:20.
2. *Mishlei* 20:18.

future behaviors.[3] I.e., will we actually refrain from repeating the sin?

To pass this test, we need an elevated level of awareness and preparation. Someone doing teshuvah is like someone who has recently recuperated from illness. Just as the recovering person has to take extra safeguards against a relapse, the person doing teshuvah must recognize his propensity to this particular sin and employ similar measures against the enticements of the Evil Inclination.[4]

Someone who is serious about becoming a different person and is not just riding the wave of the initial enthusiasm will succeed in making his teshuvah last.[5] One who wishes to be free of the sins that have clouded his relationship with God will challenge himself.

Ultimately, all efforts to change boil down to the question: Can I begin behaving in a new and improved way? Our success depends to a large degree on the strategies we employ. Our initial enthusiasm to do teshuvah will not suffice to bring us through the rough passes.[6]

In the preceding days, we gained motivation to get started on the process of teshuvah. Now, we learn practical ways to ensure that our efforts make an enduring impact on our character and our lives.

---

3. *Mishnas Rav Aharon*, Vol. 2, p. 154.

4. *Shaarei Teshuvah, Shaar* 1, *Ikar* 11

5. *Michtav MeEliyahu*, Vol. 4, p. 79.

6. Ibid.

Technique 1: Treat Causes, Not Symptoms

Rivka was depressed. Her children's antics grated on her nerves, her husband's conversation made her eyelids droop, her friend's simchas had her sitting at a table, annoyed by the music and longing for a place to nap. Nothing really touched her heart.

The parenting adviser said she should teach her children to be more cooperative. The marriage counselor said her husband should discuss things that interest her. Her rabbi said she should love her fellow Jews and feel their simchah. Each suggestion had merit, however it was her doctor who provided the strategy that solved all her problems: Get more sleep.

Most ongoing, recurring problems can be solved by seeking out their root cause. Treating the symptoms may provide temporary relief, but until the root cause is addressed, the problem will continue to resurface in new ways.

In teshuvah, the first step is to identify with crystal clarity the areas in our lives that require change. This is often no mystery to us, but even so, we tend to focus on the symptoms rather than the underlying causes.

We do so because it is easier. Quick, pragmatic results that deal with the immediate problem provide relief for the moment. Yet, when we opt for the expedient approach and deal with the symptom, rather than the cause, we can be almost certain that the situation will, in time, recur and need to be dealt with again.

That is why the laws of teshuvah require[7] that a person must forsake his "evil ways" and resolve with all his heart not to return to them again. It is not his evil *act* that he forsakes, but his *ways* — the underlying traits that lead to his wrongful acts.[8] If he does not uproot the cause of the sin, he can be sure that, when faced with the same *nisayon*,[9] he will act as he did before.

For example, at the root of *lashon hara* there may be a tendency to judge others negatively. Until a person learns to see others in a more positive light, the *lashon hara* will continue to materialize in his mind. With time, it is bound to leap from there to his tongue and out into the world.[10]

At times, because our lives are jam-packed with events, we do not discern the pattern in our situations. Without that

---

7. *Shaarei Teshuvah, Shaar* 1:11.

8. The navi (*Yeshayah* 55:7) declares, "The wicked shall give up his way, and the man of iniquity his thoughts." The verse does not say, "The wicked shall give up his deed"; rather, "The wicked shall give up his way." The verse then states, "and the man of iniquity his thoughts." A person's thoughts and his way of life are the conditions that ultimately influence his deeds. (*Nesivos Shalom*, Vol. 1, p. 209.)

9. *Matnas Chelko* on *Shaarei Teshuvah,* p. 27. See *Matnas Chaim*, Vol. 1, p. 229, s.v. *B'emes*. See also *Ohr Gedalyahu, Bereishis*, p. 29, s. v. *Keitz*.

10. Quoted from Rav Avraham Pam, heard from Rabbi Yisroel Reisman.

awareness, we do not seek out a root cause. For example, if a person does not realize that he is continually getting into disputes regarding money, he will not stop to analyze his attitude toward money to see if that is at the root of his problems.

In fact, sometimes people are fooled into thinking that the wrong direction is right for them. That is why we are commanded to choose the path of goodness and life.[11] As the Torah states, "See I have given you today life and goodness, death and evil … and you shall choose life so that you and your children may live."[12]

It's never about quick fixes, whether for nonspiritual issues such as weight loss or spiritual issues such as teshuvah. Doing teshuvah by dealing with the genesis of our misdeeds pushes us to recognize behavior patterns that do not work in our favor, to make a focused effort to relinquish those patterns, and to fill ourselves with good character traits that will leave no space for bad habits to re-emerge. Ultimately, doing teshuvah for even one sin has the power to transform the way in which we relate to ourselves, to others, and to Hashem.[13]

Points to Ponder:

- *Greatness arises from one's response to his spiritual setbacks.*

---

11. *Nesivos Shalom,* Vol. 1, p. 209.

12. *Devarim* 30:15-20.

13. See *Derech Sicha* Vol. 1, p. 616.

- *For teshuvah to be considered successful, one's future behavior must change.*

- *Techniques support our effort to make a lasting transformation.*

- *Recurring problems are often due to an unaddressed root cause.*

- *The time spent getting to the root and eradicating it is repaid in lasting change and complete teshuvah.*

לע"נ ר' אליהו שמשון ב"ר חיים צבי ז"ל

Technique 2: The Power of Resolutions

> *After years of promising himself that he would stop speaking lashon hara, Chaim gave up. "What's the point?" he thought. "I can make resolutions from here to tomorrow, but nothing ever changes."*

*C*haim may be correct, if his resolutions are mere lip service. However, if they are the result of a real awakening of his heart, accompanied by a real determination to turn over a new leaf, his resolutions are meritorious. Rabbeinu Yonah explains:[1]

> *When a person hears mussar, he should listen attentively and accept in his heart all the admonition … in a brief moment, he can go from darkness to a great light because when he hears*

---

1. *Shaarei Teshuvah, Shaar 2, Os 10.*

*and accepts all the admonition, his heart understands that he
must do teshuvah and it is as if he actually did that which he
undertakes in his heart.*

A resolution is a reality in itself. Regarding the *korban pesach*,
a verse states, "The Children of Israel went and did just as
Hashem commanded Moshe and Aaron, so did they do."[2] *Rashi*
questions how they could have already done the mitzvah when
it was commanded to them on Rosh Chodesh, two weeks before
the *korban* was to be brought.[3] He explains that as soon as the
Jews accepted the obligation, Hashem considered it done.[4]

Offering the *korban pesach*, however, was a once-a-year mitzvah. It was possible for the Jews to rally their determination at
that time. Does the same dynamic hold true for resolutions that
require long-term, sustained effort such as teshuvah?

Sustaining a *kabbalah* requires special strength. That strength
is exemplified by those who keep *shemittah*,[5] a mitzvah that
demands tremendous restraint and faith over the course of an
entire year.[6]

---

2. *Shemos* 12:28.

3. *Rashi,* citing *Mechilta.*

4. With the provision that what they accepted upon themselves was actually car-
ried out.

5. *Shemittah* teaches that our success is dependent solely on Hashem, not on
the "laws of nature." When the farmer leaves his fields fallow, he demonstrates
his belief that Hashem is the ultimate Owner of the land and that Hashem will
always provide him with all his needs.

6. Rav Chaim Shmulevitz, *Sichos Mussar, Maamar* 70, p. 304.

Those who observe *shemittah* are praised for having the strength of angels, because they make themselves impervious to the *yetzer hara*. In fact, they are greater than angels because angels are not even subject to the *yetzer hara's* appeal. Those who keep *shemittah,* on the other hand, must master their natural fears and doubts as they watch their land — their livelihood — sit untended for an entire year.[7]

This superhuman strength comes from the potency imbued by the primal *kabbalah* made by the entire Jewish people as they stood at Mount Sinai and accepted the Torah with the words "We shall do and we shall listen."[8] It is this willingness to commit ourselves to God's will, even when we are not quite sure what it will entail, that infuses our efforts with the strength of angels.

This is the "strength" we can apply to consistently practicing new behavior and thereby maintaining teshuvah over an extended period of time.[9] A *kabbalah* — to attend a *shiur,* or to count to 10 to restrain his temper, or carefully taking *maaser* from each influx of income into his household — can keep a person on track day after day.

Kabbalos are effective because they impart new levels of strength to a person.[10] When one makes a definite commitment, Hashem eases his path to assist him. These resolutions should,

7. *Vayikra Rabbah, Parshah* 1.

8. *Shabbos* 88a.

9. See *Ohr Yisroel*, Letter 7.

10. *Pe'er Hador,* Vol. 2, p. 341, cited in *Koveitz Sichos Maamar Mordechai*, Vol. 3, p. 26.

however, be employed carefully — only for flaws we are truly motivated to repair — and wisely, with realistic resolutions that we have the capacity to keep.[11]

Make It Work

Several months after the Chofetz Chaim passed away, Rabbi Elchonon Wasserman spoke to his students. He asked, 'Where did his strength lie?' Rabbi Wasserman related the following story:

> When the Chofetz Chaim was about 4 years old, he went with his friends to the marketplace. They snatched apples that had scattered from the basket of a Jewish woman vendor. Sometime later, he was studying Chumash and learned of the prohibition against stealing and the obligation to make restitution. He begged his parents for a kopeck. With that money he went to the woman, purchased several apples, and then tossed them back in the basket and ran away.
>
> Rabbi Wasserman explained, "As soon as the Chofetz Chaim's mind began to develop, he practiced what he learned. This was his greatness: whatever he learned was translated into practice."[12]

---

11. *Machsheves Mussar, Elul, Yomim Noraim,* p. 347; *Michtav MeEliyahu,* Vol. 1, p. 244.
12. *Reb Elchonon,* ArtScroll/Mesorah, p. 56.

Learning in order to "do" is the key to making enduring *kab-balos*. First, a person must internalize the need for teshuvah; he must translate his intellectual understanding into a truth in his heart. As Rav Dessler writes, "That which is acquired as truth in one's heart has influence on his actions without any stoppage or change."[13]

Despite the human tendency toward self-deception, the real truth is never completely hidden. Somewhere deep within a person, he knows the truth.[14]

Once a person's heart is set upon change, a second effective step is to put the *kabbalah* into writing. No one is too wise or too sophisticated to benefit from this step. Rabbi Chaim Ozer Grodzensky[15] wrote on Erev Yom Kippur 5694 (1933) that he had committed himself to "not become angry."[16] A handwritten *kab-balah* also has the power, when continually reviewed, to carry a person back to the moment his heart was filled with the desire to change, thereby re-inspiring him.[17]

In the final analysis, the staying power and influence of a *kabbalah* depends on the manner in which we internalize the teachings of the Torah.[18] The Chofetz Chaim's teshuvah arose from his wholehearted acceptance of what the Torah taught

---

13. *Michtav MeEliyahu,* Vol. 2, p. 56.

14. Ibid., Vol. 1, p. 61, s.v. *U'devarim.*

15. Rav of Vilna and leader of the prewar generation.

16. *Reb Elchonon,* ArtScroll/Mesorah, p. 392 .

17. *Rav Pam on the Festivals, Rabbi Sholom Smith,* ArtScroll/Mesorah, p. 41.

18. Ibid., Vol. 1, p. 60, s.v. *Biroseinu.*

him. A person who understands that Torah is teaching him how to live, finds that his resolutions to improve come from deep within his heart.[19] Rather than having to struggle to maintain his commitment, he feels happy and at peace when he does what God wants him to do.

Referring to teshuvah,[20] the Torah[21] tells us,

> *"For the commandment that I command you today is not hidden from you and it is not distant … Rather, the matter is very near to you — in your mouth and in your heart — to perform it."*

"And it is not distant": Learning Torah for knowledge alone, which produces only an intellectual understanding, leaves a person distant from a real connection with Hashem. Yet teshuvah is not meant to be distant.

"Rather, the matter is very near to you": How is it very near to you?

"In your mouth" — by studying Torah;

"And in your heart, to perform it": Torah learning that enters the heart and translates into performance of mitzvos has the power to re-shape a person's life.[22]

---

19. See *Ohr Gedalyahu, Sichos U'Maamarim, Chanukah, p. 72, s.v. L'hashkicham Torasecha.*

20. *Ramban,* Devarim 30:11.

21. Devarim 30:11,14.

22. See *Michtav Me'Eliyahu,* Vol. 1, p. 104, s.v. *U'be'emes,* which states that the way to internalize God's greatness in our heart is to make His daily miracles new in our eyes.

Points to Ponder:

- *A kabbalah has intrinsic value, apart from the mitzvah we undertake through it.*

- *Our willingness to do Hashem's will even without knowing what it will entail is "the strength of angels."*

- *This is the strength that enables us to keep our kabbalos over the long term.*

- *For a kabbalah to last, it must be felt as the truth in our hearts.*

- *Writing it down reinforces a kabbalah and reminds us of our original inspiration.*

- *Learning Torah in order to do the mitzvos, rather than for knowledge alone, leads to lasting teshuvah.*

Technique 3:
'Ein Bereirah'

Mendy was late getting home. But he knew that no matter what, Shabbos would not wait. So he hurriedly shined his shoes, showered, prepared the Shabbos lights, and checked that all else was in place. And once again, he made it on time. As always, Mendy knew that it was absolutely necessary that all his Shabbos preparations be completed on time. After all, he had no other choice! If Shabbos is coming, Shabbos is coming. Nothing else matters.

When we have no choice, we do what we must. A woman dislikes been awakened early, but she gets out of bed and tends to her early-rising toddler; she must. No one wants to "donate" a portion of their income to the government, but we all do — or else.

If we can succeed in creating an ironclad rule for ourselves that precludes sliding back into a sin, we will have given ourselves an enormously powerful tool in unlearning bad habits and learning better ones. Such a tool gives us time to solidify our new way, preventing the backsliding that often undermines our confidence and momentum.

The foundation of our entire service to Hashem is our willingness to accept the "yoke of heaven."[1] That is why the recitation of *Shema*[2] in which we commit ourselves to the "yoke of Heaven" precedes that of "*Vehayah im sha'moa*,"[3] in which we commit ourselves to obey the commandments.[4]

A *kabbalah* is the acceptance of a yoke, similar to the wooden beam placed on a pair of oxen to enable them to pull a load (oxen generally work in pairs). Once the ox is under the yoke, it *must* do its master's will. It is unable to turn around and go in another direction.

In making a *kabbalah*, we, too, need something to ensure that we stay on track. Because all beginnings are difficult and prone to setbacks, we should first make a *kabbalah*.[5]

Our own personal *kabbalos* can be fortified tremendously with this approach, called "*Ein bereirah*" (there is no choice).[6] If

---

1. *Berachos* 13a.

2. "Hear, O Israel: Hashem is our God, Hashem is the One and Only."

3. See *Tosafos* ibid. 14b, s.v. *lamah kadmah.*

4. By reciting "And it will be that if you hearken to My commandments" etc.

5. See *Koveitz Sichos Maamar Mordechai,* Vol. 3, p. 51, s.v. *Isa b'Gemara.*

6. *Michtav MeEliyahu,* Vol. 2, p. 118. s.v. *Ein shum eitzah.*

we tell ourselves, "*Ein bereirah* — I will do this, no matter what," we can acquire the Heavenly help to remove all the obstacles that lie in the path to an enduring teshuvah. This approach and the success it breeds give us the fresh beginning we need to solidify our teshuvah.

The most effective way to use the "*ein bereirah*" approach is, as mentioned earlier, to apply it to a small improvement: "No matter what, I will take a 5-minute break to call my parents every day." Then, when the *yetzer hara* begins nagging us about the chores piling up around us or the paperwork on our desk, we are armed with a reply: "I know, but I have to do this first." Giving ourselves no choice neutralizes much of the internal back-and-forth that weakens our resolve.

Once we see that we are able to enforce our decisions upon ourselves in smaller matters, we gain the strength to tackle larger matters. With a *kabbalah* of "necessity," the evil inclination cannot rule.[7] "*Ein bereirah*" works.

Technique 4: Easy Does It

Leah found her job difficult and daunting, but needed the income, and there were no other foreseeable options. Therefore,

---

7. *Daas Chochmah U'Mussar,* beginning of Vol. 2, cited in *Kovetz Sichos Maamar Mordechai,* Vol. 3, p. 28, s.v. *V'chain gam;* p. 52, s.v. *Ach adayin.*

Leah woke up each morning, did her morning routines, got into her car, and drove to her taxing job.

There were two routes: the highway or a winding, country road dotted with farmhouses and gardens, and shaded by majestic oak trees. Invariably, Leah took the scenic route. The prospect of the soothing drive made each and every day more tolerable.

*T*eshuvah can be challenging. Setting out on a new road can be daunting. Most of us often face several areas where there is need for improvement. For example, a man is likely to feel that he should put more time and effort into learning Torah. He may realize that, in general, he does not utilize his time properly. He may be careless when making a *berachah*. He may detect flaws in his relationships with his wife and children. He may wish he were more helpful to his shul and community.

With such a giant task laid out before us, how can we even begin? At times, we feel overwhelmed and full of self-doubt. Therefore, it is advisable to "take the scenic route," that is, to find the area of improvement that is most pleasing to our hearts, and start with that. [8]

8. Rav Dessler (*Sefer HaZikaron L'Baal Michtav MeEliyahu,* Vol. 2, p. 155) advises that a person trying to change a habit and succeed in teshuvah should set his sights on something taxing — but not overwhelming — by setting a "minimum" and a "maximum" goal. The minimum goals is that within reach. The maximum goal is the vision toward which he strives.

King Solomon advises, "Follow the path of your heart."[9] The first thrust when doing teshuvah should be to improve in the area(s) toward which a person feels a natural pull.[10] Thus, if his natural bent is in the area of Torah study, his teshuvah should begin in Torah study. If it is in human relations, then he should begin teshuvah in that area.

The danger in beginning our teshuvah process with something that we find difficult is that we might encounter frustration that will end up halting the process in its tracks.[11] On the other hand, if we succeed at the first level of self-improvement, our desire to do teshuvah expands: change is possible! Even a minor success can catapult us forward on our quest to reach our full potential.

> *A young man was discouraged by the fact that for many years, he had been unable to defeat the Evil Inclination. One day he read advice in one of Rabbi Yisroel Salanter's letters that changed his life. Rabbi Salanter would encourage people trying to overcome the Evil Inclination to begin with the easiest thing. With great confidence he took the advice and began his ascent.[12]*

---

9. *Koheles* 11:9.

10. Netziv, *Haamek Davar,* end of *Parashas Shelach.*

11. *Ohr Yisroel, Siman* 15. See *Michtav Me'Eliyahu,* Vol. 5, p. 375, which states that a person should not strive for a level that is too far above his present status. Otherwise, he is setting himself up for failure and despair.

12. *Aleinu L'Shabei'ach, Vayikra,* Introduction, p. 17.

Once a person's teshuvah *succeeds* in matters that are near and dear to him, he is poised to address the next area that needs attention.[13] By analyzing the successes and duplicating the steps he took to succeed and by not dwelling on the setbacks, he paves the way for future success.

Points to Ponder:

- *Teshuvah can seem like a daunting, overwhelming task.*

- *A powerful technique for enforcing our own kabbalos is to tell ourselves, "Ein bereirah — there is no choice."*

- *By that means we close down all the yetzer hara's argument against our kabbalah, telling ourselves that we really have no choice but to keep it.*

- *Success in the "easy" matters strengthens us to tackle difficult ones.*

- *Ein bereirah is most effective when it is first applied to small kabbalos. Then we can build on that success to take on larger changes.*

---

13. Rav Pam, *The Pleasant Way,* by Rabbi Sholom Smith, p. 241.

Technique 5:
Read the Manual

Danny considered himself a fairly handy person. So when he purchased a brand new, state-of-the-art cell-phone, he cast the instruction manual aside and began pressing buttons. Hours later, when he still hadn't installed his contact list, set his ring-tone, or located the shutter button for the camera, he abashedly picked up the manual and began reading.

*G*enerally, the more complex the mechanism, the greater is the need to read the instructions. In the observance of mitzvos, the halachos (laws) are the instruction manual that teach us how to ensure that we "press all the right buttons" to bring about the spiritual benefits each mitzvah engenders.

Proper speech, Shabbos observance, business dealings, and prayer are just a few of the areas of a Jew's everyday life that are governed by halachah. It is impossible to correct the mistakes and sins we commit in these areas unless we know the applicable laws of teshuvah.

For instance, one may study mussar regarding *lashon hara* and become very inspired to improve, but inspiration alone is not enough to prevent him from stumbling.

"There is no solution other than studying halachah, just as one learns the laws regarding stealing, *kashrus*, etc.,"[1] says the Chofetz Chaim. He teaches:

> *Most people who fail regarding lashon hara do so because of a lack of knowledge [of its laws]. [The only solution] for this deficiency is to first learn the particulars of the prohibition against speaking lashon hara.*[2]

Learning should be consistent and methodical, he advises. "There must be a set time each day, whether a lot or a little, to learn the laws and the mussar relevant to speech."[3]

For many other mitzvos as well, it is virtually impossible to observe the mitzvah without studying its laws. Therefore, we stand to lose the great merit we could acquire by doing the mitzvah properly.

Chofetz Chaim[4] highlights the great reward for proper

---

1. *Kuntres Kevod Shamayim, Pesichah,* s.v. *V'kaasher yisbonein.*

2. *Shemiras HaLashon, Shaar HaTevunah,* Ch. 16 , s.v. *U'Ve'emes kimat.*

3. *Chovas HeShemirah,* Ch. 3, cited in *Kovetz Sichos Maamar Mordechai,* Vol. 1, p. 24. See *Inspiration and Insight,* Vol. 1, Translated and Arranged by *Rabbi Shimon Finkelman,* ArtScroll/Mesorah p. 52.

4. Preface to *Mishnah Berurah* (Vol. 3).

Shabbos observance: "Whoever keeps Shabbos in accordance with its laws will have his sins forgiven."[5] This can only be achieved, however, with a thorough knowledge of the laws of Shabbos.[6]

For a person who struggles with dishonesty, learning the laws imparts a sense of the seriousness of these types of sins and the gravity of the punishments associated with them. Through this knowledge, the person who engages in trickery, lying, stealing, or similar sins can find motivation to change. [7]

When the Torah tells us that teshuvah is "in your mouth and in your heart,"[8] it is emphasizing that we should study the laws of teshuvah. In this way, we infuse the mitzvah of teshuvah "with flavor."[9] We are then able to do it enthusiastically and properly, and reap the rich rewards teshuvah always brings.

Getting Through

Benjie was in the middle of telling his brother Zev a long, involved story over the telephone. After a while, he realized that he no longer heard the "uh-huh" and "really?" and "wow!"

---

5. *Shabbos* 118b.
6. Chida in *Nachal Kodmim,* cited in *Aleinu L'Shabei'ach, Devarim,* p. 264.
7. See *Rashi* on *Avos* 2:5.
8. *Devarim* 30:11,14; see *Ramban* ibid. v. 14.
9. *Derech Sichah,* Vol. 2, p. 218.

with which his brother punctuated the tale. "Zev? Zev? Are you there?" Benjie said. No answer. The connection had been severed. How long had he been talking to himself, he wondered.

*I*magine if, Heaven forbid, a person's prayers were disconnected from Hashem. What a waste of his prayers potential!

Yet without a grasp of the halachos of prayer, this scenario can indeed be the outcome. It would seem to be implausible that given prayer's essential role in bringing every aspect of Hashem's goodness into our world, a person would be lax in learning how to properly pray.

Nevertheless, the Talmud[10] states that prayer is among "things that stand at the pinnacle of the world but which people treat lightly." That "light treatment" must be dispelled before a person can get back on track and learn the halachos he needs to know in order to pray effectively.

Rav Mattisyahu Salomon[11] advises:

> *If we want our prayers to be effective, we must first clear our record … Only after we ask forgiveness for our neglect and abuse of prayer can we expect God to accept our prayers.*[12]

Once we have rid ourselves of any faulty attitudes toward prayer, learning the laws of prayer ensures that our future

---

10. See *Berachos* 6b with *Rashi*.

11. *Matnas Chaim*, Vol. 2, p. 29, s.v. *V'im kein*.

12. *With Hearts Full of Faith*, by *Rabbi Mattisyahu Salomon*, Adapted for Print by Rabbi Yaakov Yosef Reinman, ArtScroll/Mesorah, p. 100.

approach will be correct and our prayers will therefore be heard. Rav Salomon continues:

> *Who knows if it is because we are missing the laws [of tefillah] our prayers are not accepted … By carrying out the halachos one can come closer to prayer with kavannah that will ensure that his prayers will be heard …* [13]

Learning the halachos in any area of Jewish life is so significant that where the opportunity to perform a mitzvah is not available, we are considered to have fulfilled it by learning its laws.[14] Learning halachah has the power to change a person, just as bringing an offering in the *Beis HaMikdash* was intended to change a person: to inspire him to rectify bad behavior and character.

Rabbi Shlome Wolbe[15] sums it up, "The most essential ingredient in any successful teshuvah program is Torah knowledge."

Points to Ponder:

- *Teshuvah, like every other mitzvah, can only be done properly by learning the related halachos.*

---

13. *Matnas Chaim,* Vol. 2, p. 29, s.v. *V'Im Kein;* see *Orach Chaim Siman* 94:1.

14. *Menachos* 110a. This is the law [Torah] of the elevation offering when we have no Beis HaMikdash — we can involve ourselves in Torah study, and it as if we brought an offering.

15. *Alei Shur* Vol. 1, p. 236.

- *Learning the laws of Shabbos can bring forgiveness for all sins.*

- *Our prayers are not heard when we abuse and neglect our power of prayer.*

- *When one person cannot perform a mitzvah, his learning its halachah is counted as if he has actually performed it.*

Technique 6:
Set Safeguards

Joshua is susceptible to bronchitis. Whenever he catches a cold, he is bedridden with fever and a deep, racking cough. Therefore, he must be extremely careful about exposing himself to cold germs. He washes his hands frequently, shys away from those who cough and sneeze, and swallows a megadose of vitamin C every day. He knows that if he lowers his vigilance, he is likely to become seriously ill.

In the same way, a person who is susceptible to a certain sin or temptation has to enact safeguards that a less susceptible person may not require. He has already determined that he has a certain area of weakness. Upon recovering from that spiritual malady through teshuvah, he has to protect himself from its recurrence.[1]

---

1. *Shaarei Teshuvah, Shaar* 1, *Ikar* 11.

Each of us can benefit from erecting personal boundaries specific to our needs.[2] For example, to stop speaking *lashon hara*, we are told to limit saying even complimentary things about other people[3] who are not in our presence, unless absolutely necessary (i.e., *shidduch* information). This creates an effective safeguard against speaking ill about someone.

The verse[4] states: "You shall safeguard My charge that these abominable traditions that were done before you not be done, and not make yourselves impure through them. I am Hashem, your God." The Talmud derives the concept of erecting a fence around the Torah from this exhortation to safeguard the commandments. For example, Shabbos observance is, in many instances, defined by the Rabbinic enactments that "safeguard" the basic prohibitions of labor.[5]

Safeguards most often entail distancing ourselves from the people, places, or situations that lead us to sin.[6] For example, Rabbeinu Yonah[7] cites 24 conditions that will obstruct a per-

---

2. *Mesillas Yesharim,* Ch. 13, s.v.. *Haperishos; V'im tishal.*

3. *Bava Basra* 164b; *Hilchos Lashon Hara, Klal 9, Siman* 1.

4. *Vayikra* 18:30.

5. *Shaarei Teshuvah,* end of *Shaar* 1.

6. *Mesillas Yesharim,* Ch. 14, states there are three types of "*perishus,*", separates epitomized in the words of the *Talmud* (*Yevamos* 20a): "Sanctify yourself through what is permitted to you" (see *Takanos HaShavim, Siman* 9, s.v. v'*hahagdaros b'mutar*), there are abstentions from the pleasures of this world to ensure that one does not involve himself in sin itself (*Mesillas Yesharim,* s.v. *Haperishos*); separations in "*dinim,*" stringencies, and creating a "fence" in Jewish law (*Sanhedrin* 19a, *Rashi* s.v. *Mikedushaso lo yeitzei).*

7. *Hilchos Teshuvah.*

son's efforts at teshuvah. The fifth condition is "associating with wrongdoers." If we do not separate ourselves from those who relish their lives of overindulgence and sin, our perspective becomes skewed. We hear so much about their activities that we become desensitized to the sinfulness and repercussions of this type of life. We fall prey to the notion that the only way to fit in socially with such friends is to do as they do.

For failings that require long-term teshuvah, such as changing a bad characteristic,[8] safeguards are particularly useful. In general, bad character and bad habits have "triggers." For example, the trigger might be a certain person who provokes an angry, aggressive response. It might be a specific tension-producing activity, such as driving in heavy traffic.

When the triggers of bad habits occur, it is extremely difficult to stop the negative response in its tracks. One solution is to set safeguards. As much as possible, avoid the environment that trips the trigger. Avoid traffic by taking a less-traveled road. Limit your interactions with the person who irritates you, or if that is not feasible, prepare a more acceptable response to him.

By setting up safeguards, we reduce the number of times our teshuvah is tested. We give ourselves time to build up good habits in situations that are easier for us to handle, making it more likely that we will succeed when the triggers are set off again.

We often find that a character problem is correctable by changing the environment that evokes the problematic trait.

8. See *Rambam, Hilchos Dei'os* 2:3.

Even small adjustments can lead to dramatic changes in behavior. Safeguards enable us to maintain our teshuvah without having to wrestle our *yetzer hara* to the ground each and every time.

Technique 7: Take Action

As an intelligent, thinking, being, man has all types of thoughts flashing constantly through his mind. Even sublime thoughts of remorse and self-improvement are not strange to him, yet, they are often fleeting. For his thoughts to have lasting meaning, he must ultimately convert them into action.

As we have already learned, the Torah teaches us the nature of teshuvah in the verse:

> *For the commandment that I command you today is not hidden from you and it is not distant … Rather, the matter is very near to you — in your mouth and your heart — to perform it.*[9]

The words "to perform it," says the Kotzker Rebbe, teach us that teshuvah must be translated into our actions. Just thinking, feeling and saying the right things does not fulfill the mitzvah.

Actions are imperative because what we do has a profound effect upon ourselves as well as on those around us. *Doing*

---

9. *Devarim* 30:11,14.

better invariably leads to *being* better. In the realm of sin, our first step is to realize the damage caused by our deeds, and to theretofore act differently. Even if we do not feel differently — i.e., we still find a certain person irritating — teshuvah demands that we treat the person with patience and respect, meanwhile working on improving our internal feelings.[10]

Let us focus on a profound psychological insight: When we act a certain way — whatever our intentions — we are influenced by those actions, which eventually changes our thoughts and emotions. People who engage in negative activities, even if at first it is not heartfelt, will eventually become negative people. In contradistinction, those who "fake" smiles and kindness will eventually feel friendly and kind.[11]

Therefore, we have to approach specific sins with specific corrective actions,[12] targeting the problematic area.[13] For instance, someone who has difficulty keeping his gaze from impure sights can take action by averting his eyes when something improper comes into view. Someone who speaks *lashon hara* can take action by speaking positively.

Through action, we can recommit our physical selves to doing Hashem's will.

---

10. *Michtav Me'Eliyahu,* Vol. 5, p. 236, s.v. *Ulam.*
11. See *Sefer HaChinuch* Mitzvah 16.
12. *Shaarei Teshuvah* 1:35.
13. *Vayikra Rabbah* 21:5; *Tanchuma, Parashas Beshalach* 24; *Rambam, Hilchos Dei'os* 2:2. See *Tzidkas HaTzaddik, Simanim* 49, 255.

Legs that ran to commit a sin can run to a mitzvah. A tongue that spoke lies can speak words of truth, wisdom and chesed. Hands that have hurt others can be opened to help the poor. Someone who has stirred arguments among people, can bring peace among people.[14]

Ultimately, each positive action we perform will help concretize the feelings motivating our teshuvah. The Patriarchs performed mitzvos before the Torah was given to the Jewish people. By doing so, their spiritual awakening was translated into action and became a permanent part of their lives.[15]

This technique is crucial in ensuring that there is a true and lasting awakening of teshuvah. Thoughts that do not lead to action are lacking a necessary component. Taking action is the completion of the thought, and an essential step in our efforts to turn our teshuvah into a lasting elevation.[16]

Points to Ponder:

- *When a person knows his weakness, he can safeguard himself against it.*

---

14. See *Shemiras Halashon, Shaar HaZechirah,* end of Ch. 13. See also *Derech Sichah,* Vol. 1, p. 626.

15. *Ohr Gedalyahu, Shemos,* p. 86, fn. 3, citing *Noam Elimelech. Ramban* (ibid.) explains that once a person experiences an awakening and longing to do good, if he wants that feeling to remain, he must concretize his desire into action.

16. *Ohr Gedalyahu, Bereishis,* p. 51.

- *Safeguards often entail separating ourselves from that which provokes our transgression.*

- *Safeguards help a person train himself away from bad character traits.*

- *Taking action on the thoughts of teshuvah is a necessary step to make teshuvah enduring.*

- *Thoughts that do not lead to action are incomplete.*

- *Even when someone acts in a way that is actually more elevated than his true feelings, the influence of his actions will help to elevate his feelings.*

Technique 8: Develop Positive Habits

> *For his first day of kindergarten, Gavriel wanted to go to the bus stop in his old blue jacket. It was a strange, scary day, and the 4-year-old wanted to be bundled in the comfort of the soft, faded jacket he had worn for the past year.*
>
> *"But I bought you this beautiful new green jacket!" his mother protested. "The blue one is so small on you, and there's a big rip on the sleeve. You don't want to go to your new school like that!"*
>
> *The little boy insisted, tears streaming down his cheeks, that he could not get on the bus in anything but his trusted blue jacket. Perplexed, yet wary of turning his first day into a struggle, his mother relented.*

No matter how badly they fit, no matter how poorly they serve us, our old habits are as comfortable as an old jacket. We slip into them naturally without any effort. Even when we know we are doing something harmful to ourselves or others, on a certain level, we are attached to our old habits. Therefore, it may be difficult to imagine shedding them.

Change requires a period of adjustment before a new habit feels like our own. That period is fraught with danger of a setback. We feel at odds with our new way of doing things — the benefits have not yet fully emerged — and we miss our old familiar way. In that interim state, motivation may be difficult to sustain.

Rambam[1] teaches that "among the paths of repentance is for the penitent to separate himself from the object of his sin and to change his behavior ... to the good."

This means that a person can harness the power of habit and use it to serve Hashem by "changing his behavior ... to the good," even for actions that are not sins.[2] Making such a change proves to us that change is possible, and this in turn fuels our confidence that we can succeed in coming closer to Hashem with complete teshuvah that endures.[3]

In fact, we pray for positive habits every day after the morning blessings: *"She'targileinu b'sorasecha* — that You accustom us to [study] Your Torah." We are not only asking for the opportunity to study, but for this to become our natural, default activity.

---

1. *Hilchos Teshuvah* 2:4.
2. *Sifsei Chaim*, *Moadim*, Vol. 1, p. 61.
3. Ibid.

Positive habits, while more difficult to acquire, are every bit as powerful as their negative counterparts. Setting a goal is the first step. A person can then begin moving toward that goal, repeating each step until the new habit becomes familiar. For example, a person who wishes to say *berachos* with more *kavannah* can start by just focusing on the word "*baruch* — Hashem is a wellspring of blessings."[4] When that becomes ingrained, he can move onto *"Ata"* — we beseech Hashem directly[5] and so forth, until saying *berachos* with meaning and concentration becomes his new reality.[6]

Force of habit is just that: a force. It is in fact a tremendous force with which every person must reckon whenever he sets out to improve himself. Each time a person repeats an action, he builds a driving momentum behind it that moves it forward on its own power. Like a strong wind at a sprinter's back, momentum can propel a person to the finish line with far greater speed and ease than his own efforts could produce.[7]

Negative habits can be overturned and replaced with new positive habits. Just as a habit can drain a person's life it can be the tool that refills it to overflowing. For both good and bad, *"hergel na'aseh teva"* — habit becomes second nature.

---

4. For elucidation on the meaning of "*baruch,*" *see Praying with Fire* Day 28 p.110.
5. *She'eilos U'Teshuvos Ha'Rashba,* Vol. 5, *Siman* 52; *Yesod V'Shoresh HaAvodah;* also cited in *Halichos Shlomo (Tefillah), p. 362, s.v. Yeish davar m'yuchad.*
6. See *Michtav MeEliyahu,* Vol. 1, p. 25. Also see *Shemiras HaLashon,* Introduction, Days 7-9.
7. See *Sifsei Chaim, Moadim,* Vol. 1, p. 61.

Technique 9: Keep a Journal

The crowd listened to the candidate's speech. Within a few hours, however, most had forgotten much of what he had said. That is, except for the journalists. They had written down every important phrase, and before the day was done, formulated the thoughts into an article for the next day's newspaper.

When you know you have to write some thing down, you pay close attention. When you know you will be called upon to make sense of what has happened, you analyze and synthesize the information as you hear it.

When we decide to do teshuvah, we need to pay careful attention to what goes on around us and within us each day. A good way to guarantee this seriousness of purpose is to keep a journal in which we can track the progress of our efforts at self-improvement. In doing so, we find that rather than passing by in a blur, our days and our activities within each day become more meaningful.

Rabbeinu Yonah[8] advises that keeping a written record in which we note every slip up and every triumph, big or small, greatly assists our effort to improve. Since everyone, no matter how righteous, commits a multitude of sins throughout the year, this exercise reminds us of the areas that need the most work.

---

8. *Shaarei Teshuvah, Shaar* 1:8

It demonstrates, also, that authentic teshuvah is an unending, lifelong quest.

A journal detailing each day's progress is best written at the end of that day. To make the journal a methodical record of progress, a separate section should be designated for each trait: for instance, patience, sensitivity, and generosity.

In each section, the person should write down everything he did or said that day pertaining to these traits. Was there a particular *nisayon* in any of these areas? How did he react? What might he have done differently?

The following guidelines make this journal a vital, useful tool:

- Write everything down. Don't wait for an important event. Every day is important and can serve to strengthen our efforts.
- Say as much as you want, at as much length as you want. Writing skills do not matter.
- Remember that your journal is private. The more candid and complete your record is, the more helpful it will be in your effort to improve yourself.
- Focus as closely on your triumphs and positive actions as you do on your misdeeds. Recognize how you have improved in each trait, how you handled a situation today better than you would have a month ago. Even the worst day has several bright spots; record them.

Every journal should also have a place to record the things for which we are grateful to Hashem on that day. Not only is this a meritorious practice, but it is a powerful fuel for all of our teshuvah. As *Chovos HaLevavos*[9] teaches, "through recognizing Hashem's goodness a person comes to serve God."[10]

> *There is not a single person who will fail to recognize his indebtedness to his Creator. And when he observes the benevolence that Hashem has bestowed upon him, he will surely be inspired to alacrity in his service of Hashem.*[11]

Points to Ponder:

- *Even harmful habits are difficult to shed.*
- *Good habits can be built up, step by step, to replace those that are harmful.*
- *When positive actions become habit, they, too, become "second nature."*
- *One should write down everything with candor so that he can make a sincere analysis of his actions.*
- *Writing the day's events and actions enables us to analyze our progress in self-improvement.*
- *Making special note of reasons to be grateful to Hashem motivates us to serve Him better.*

---

9. *Shaar HaBechinah.*
10. *Mesillas Yesharim*, Ch. 8. See *Siddur R' Yaakov Emden* (Halachos after Maariv 2,4).
11. *Mesillas Yesharim*, ibid.

Technique 10:
Visualize Success

*D*o you want to be even better? Do you wish you were that parent who seems so relaxed and affectionate with his own children? Do you wish you were the person who feels some of the sanctity of Shabbos?

Perhaps these pictures do not fully capture your aspirations for yourself, but there is no doubt that *some* picture does. You know how you *wish* you had handled your challenges, how you *wish* you had reacted to others, how you *wish* you had spent your time more wisely.

Visualization is a powerful way of jump-starting your ascent to these elevated versions of yourself. It is not dreaming; it is formulating a new self, starting in your imagination and then, inevitably, spreading to your thoughts and actions.

We all know how real the products of our imaginations can be. If we imagine that a noise in the night is a burglar, our hearts start pounding and every creak and squeak builds our sense of panic. This is true even if the house is as locked up and well alarmed as a bank vault. Our imagined woes take on the full power of real woes, evoking the same physical and mental reactions.

The same power, used purposefully, can help us become who we want to be:

> *Picture yourself in a situation that normally evokes a negative trait you would like to change. Then, picture yourself engaged in your bad habit. Visualize your usual response to the situation, and feel fully the guilt or frustration aroused by your action. Think of how this looks from the outside, or more importantly, from Above.*
>
> *Now replay the scene, but this time, react as you would like to. Imagine yourself exercising self-control, being dignified and gracious. Fully feel the sense of accomplishment and mastery your new reaction builds within you. Focus on how happy Hashem will be due to your new behavior.*

It is important to actually visualize these two scenes so that your emotions will be moved. The shame you feel in the first image and the self-respect and pride you feel in the second image will keep you motivated.

It is most effective to do these visualization exercises when you are about to enter a situation to which they apply. For instance, if a mother has trouble being patient with her children, she should visualize her interactions with them right before they walk through the door at the end of the school day.

Although the gap between who we are and who we want to

be appears wide, visualization is something concrete we can each do to bridge the gap. Our visualization is like an architect's rendering. It shows us what we will have created when we complete the difficult, disruptive renovation job, and that is what keeps us going.

In addition, visualization allows us to rehearse the new thoughts, words, and deeds that will formulate our new selves. With enough practice, we will be able to turn these mental rehearsals into a real, virtuoso performance.

In the lessons we have learned throughout this 40-day journey, we have encountered teshuvah as a Torah obligation, as a self-improvement plan, as a practical matter and as a matter of the soul. We have learned strategies to convince ourselves to jump over the hurdles and try to change, and technigues to ensure that we can sustain our efforts for the long haul.

In its truest sense, teshuvah is not a laborious journey. Rather, teshuvah is a treasure to pursue, for nothing ensures us more joy than a vibrant, enduring connection to our Creator. May we each merit this unparalleled gift, and may all of Klal Yisrael be blessed with a year of good health, prosperity, happiness, security, and peace. May Hashem speedily bring the *Geulah*.

Points to Ponder:

- *To use visualization toward teshuvah, we should imagine ourselves acting in our negative manner, and then imagine ourselves acting as we would like to.*

- *We should allow ourselves to fully feel the shame of our first scenario and the dignity and self-respect of the second.*

- *These mental exercises motivate us to change, and help us to rehearse better responses to our challenges.*

- *Teshuvah is an obligation that demands much effort. At its core, however, it is a valuable gift that bestows upon us the greatest joy attainable: a clear connection to our Creator.*

LAWS

Halachos:
The Laws of
Teshuvah

LAWS
I

Levels of Teshuvah

*W*hile all teshuvah is valuable, not all teshuvah is equal. The power of our teshuvah corresponds to the emotional and spiritual depth from which it emerges. In teshuvah, the purest water is drawn from the deepest well. Nevertheless, the curative power of teshuvah begins when we first reach into our hearts to begin the process.[1]

The Talmud[2] discusses two seemingly conflicting verses that illustrate that our status is elevated the moment we initiate an effort to return to Hashem. The first verse states, "Do I desire the death of the wicked [man] . . ."[3] The second states, "For Hashem desired to kill them."[4] The Talmud reconciles the disparity, explaining that the first verse refers to those who are inclined to do teshuvah. Therefore, even though they are termed "wicked,"

---

1. See *Michtav MeEliyahu*, Vol. 2, page 78, s.v. *Aval hisoreorus*.
2. *Niddah* 70b.
3. *Yechezkeil* 18:23.
4. *I Shmuel* 2:25.

God does not desire their death. The second verse, on the other hand, refers to those who have no inclination to repent.[5]

If the person in the first verse is still called "wicked," we may wonder why his inclination toward teshuvah is enough to make him worthy of continued life. The answer is that the person has only begun the teshuvah process. As a result of that small effort however, God reckons him as a *"baal teshuvah"* and allots him the additional years needed to complete the teshuvah process.[6] God encourages this man's teshuvah proactively, giving him inspiration to return.[7] In the second verse, regarding those who have no inclination to repent, God's encouragements will not occur.

The infamous King Achav illustrates the transforming power of even incomplete teshuvah. His teshuvah was far from complete, and yet God told the prophet Eliyahu,[8] "Have you seen that Achav is submissive to Me? Because he has humbled himself before Me, I will not bring the disaster in his days."[9]

Earning a completely clean slate requires maximum effort. The sin-stained soul is like a soiled white shirt. With a superficial washing, only the surface dirt is loosened. It takes a deep, thorough cleaning, with stain remover scrubbed into the tough

---

5. See *Malbim* on *I Shmuel* 2:25, which states that this does not mean that Hashem removes the person's free will. Rather, Hashem will offer no assistance.

6. *Ohr Yisroel, Siman* 30, s.v. *Mah yachil,* cited in *Mishnas Rav Aharon*, Vol. 4, p. 101, s.v. *V'HaInyan bazeh; Matnas Chelko* on *Shaarei Teshuvah*, p. 35.

7. *Malbim* on *I Shmuel* 2:25.

8. *I Melachim* 21:29.

9. See *Matnas Chelko*, on *Shaarei Teshuvah*, p. 52.

spots, for the shirt to emerge impeccably white.[10] But when that soul emerges from the "wash," the feeling is one of pure lightness and joy as King David describes: "Happy is the man unto whom Hashem counts not iniquity, and in whose spirit there is no guile."[11]

Why settle for a "superficial wash" when the reward for a complete teshuvah is so much greater? We are motivated to embark on a rigorous road of complete repentance only when our heart is so sensitive that it feels great discomfort because we have sinned.[12] Such a response comes from a refined, enlightened soul, and the grief that such a person feels serves as atonement for his wrong.[13] In fact, God desires this broken heart to any other kind of atonement, "for it proceeds from the purification of the heavenly soul."

A person's spiritual stature can be measured by the degree to which he actively engages in teshuvah, thereby drawing closer to God. Yet, wherever we begin on the ladder of teshuvah, it is certain that our desire to reconnect to God will take us upward, sensitizing our souls and bringing us closer to the pure happiness of "the man unto whom God counts no iniquity."

---

10. *Shaarei Teshuvah, Shaar* 1:9.

11. *Tehillim* 32:2.

12. *Shaarei Teshuvah, Shaar* 1:13.

13. One who does a sin and is embarrassed by it, God will forgive him" (*Berachos* 12b).

Points to Ponder:

- *Once a person begins teshuvah, God considers him a baal teshuvah and allots him time to complete his repentance.*

- *An enlightened, refined person feels great pain when he sins. That pain is considered the greatest atonement.*

- *Each step in teshuvah brings a person closer to this enlightened, refined state.*

Step One on the Road to Teshuvah

As the burglar slipped out the back door of the house, he had a surprise waiting for him. A passing patrol car had noticed something suspicious, and now two armed policemen stopped the thief in his tracks. The burglar quickly regretted his decision to rob the house. Why did he pick this neighborhood? Why had he chosen a moonlit night? Why did he decide on this corner house, where his presence had a better chance of being observed?

The burglar was full of regret. But it was not regret that would move him to abandon his life of crime. Rather, it would simply move him to be more careful next time, so that his crime could succeed.

People often have regret. Not because they feel they were wrong, but simply because their actions have thrust them into an unpleasant situation they would rather have avoided.

Without real regret, heartfelt teshuvah cannot get off the

ground.[1] Although *Rabbeinu Yonah*[2] lists twenty components of repentance, he relates that "Teshuvah is based on three main components, without which the service of teshuvah is not possible ... They are: regret, abandoning sin, and verbal confession."[3]

Unless a person recognizes he is doing wrong, he cannot begin to reform. A twinge of guilt is a wake up call without which the person's conscience remains asleep.

For example, one who grows up in a non-observant home will not feel guilt eating cheeseburgers, and will continue to eat them. However, one who grows up in a strictly kosher home might feel guilt even when eating kosher, if it is not up to his usual accepted standard of kashrus. His guilt prods him to examine why he succumbed to the temptation. Was it his craving for the food? Social pressure? Being too lazy to walk to a restaurant with his standards of kashrus? When he regrets having succumbed to the weakness and "offending" God, that opens the door to growth.

Regret is generally considered the first step[4] in the teshuvah process.[5] There has to be real remorse in a person's

---

1. *Michtav MeEliyahu*, Vol. 2, p. 79, s.v. *Amnam*.

2. *Shaarei Teshuvah*, *Shaar* 1.

3. *Shaarei Teshuvah*, 1:19. See *Kli Yakar, Devarim* 30:11. See *Yoma* 85b that one cannot say in advance, "I can do this sin, then do teshuvah, and He will forgive me . . ."

4. See *Beis Elokim, Shaar HaTeshuvah*, Chapter 2, s.v. *U'milas teshuvah*.

5. See *Matnas Chelko*, on *Shaarei Teshuvah, p.* 21. See *Shaarei Teshuvah* 1:11, which states that where a person clings to the negative action, forsaking one's "evil ways" must precede regret.

heart.[6] When we think about what we have done, we should feel, without reservations, "I wish I could rewind this film and do it over again differently."

Part of that sense of regret springs from fear; there is an acute realization that God is watching and meting out justice, and that no unrepented sin goes unpunished.[7] A more elevated sense of regret, however, comes from understanding the impact of our misdeeds on our own soul and on our relationship with God. We wonder: Why have we done this to the beautiful, pure soul Hashem has given us; why have we placed a barrier between our Creator and us? Why have we diminished our share in the World to Come?

Like a parent who has turned away from his child for that one crucial moment in which the child is injured, our regret comes to us in the words, "What have I done?" That is the level of remorse that sets off the mechanisms of teshuvah and strengthens the commitment to make a permanent change.[8]

In Western society, regret is often regarded as a mentally unhealthy state. For a Jew, however, regret is the necessary awakening that allows spiritual accomplishments to soar. As much as we would love to stay comfortably asleep, we know that it is only by rising and taking on the day that we can enjoy the thrill of achievement.

---

6. *Michtav MeEliyahu*, Vol. 2, p. 79, s.v. *Amnam*.

7. *Shaarei Teshuvah, Shaar* 1:10. See there that *Rabbeinu Yonah*, ibid., mentions seven aspects that are involved in having regret.

8. *Michtav MeEliyahu*, Vol. 2, p. 79.

Points to Ponder:

- *Although it is an emotionally uncomfortable state, regret is the necessary catalyst to real teshuvah.*

- *Regret stems from two sources: awareness of Hashem's judgment, and dismay at having caused distance between one's soul and Hashem.*

That Lingering Odor

Mike loved garlic. One day, he volunteered to make dinner for the family: a big pot of spaghetti with a special garlic sauce. He peeled and crushed four whole heads of garlic and added them to the simmering sauce on the stove.

Everyone enjoyed the spicy sauce, especially Mike. But the second he finished dinner, he remembered that he was scheduled to attend a meeting for his son's yeshivah.

"You should wash your hands," his wife suggested. "You smell like garlic."

"Gotta run," he replied on his way out the door.

As the meeting convened a short while later, Mike noticed a few people sniffing the air suspiciously. "What's that odor?" one asked another. "I don't know. It smells gross."

A person who sins, but never regrets doing the sin, never quite rids himself of its lingering "odor." That is why it is not enough to think, "What's past is past. I'll just make sure I never do it again."

Regret of the past is a necessary element of complete teshuvah, because "the past must be repaired." [1] Before a dentist fills a cavity, he drills to remove the decay. Otherwise, beneath the shiny new filling, bacteria will continue to eat away at the tooth. This is the way of the physical world, and to an even greater degree, it is the way of the spiritual world as well.

But why does teshuvah follow this pattern? If a person commits himself to never revisit his sin, why can he not declare himself free of it and move forward from there? Isn't that what renewal is really all about? Especially for a sin that has no victim warranting reparation, why is it beneficial to arouse our hearts to regret that which we did?

The fact is that although the sin may seem to be expunged without regret, it is not. Like the unpleasant odor in the opening story, the sin clings to the person, creating an invisible barrier between himself and God, between his desire to reach higher levels of spirituality and his ability to do so.

This occurs because in the world of spirituality, time does not exist in the linear, cause-and-effect way that it exists in this world. There is no concept of past, present, and future, but rather, in some manner, it all exists simultaneously. The sin,

---

1. *Michtav MeEliyahu*, Vol. 2, p. 79, s.v. *Amnam lo.*

unless erased by sincere regret, still exists and adheres to the sinner. As a result, he will experience terrible frustration in his spiritual efforts.

Although human nature is to forget about past unpleasantness, in spiritual matters, the effect of the past is not diminished even one iota, until we experience regret. We see this concept in the Torah's words regarding intentional idolatry: "He blasphemed Hashem — the person shall be cut off from among his people, for he scorned the word of Hashem and broke His commandment; that person will surely be cut off, his sin is upon him."[2] Even after death, the spiritual corruption of the sin cleaves to the soul and keeps it from the World to Come.[3]

Fortunately, the situation is not hopeless; the soul is cut off only as long as there is no teshuvah.[4] Repentance removes the sin and the punishment.

Teshuvah demands rebuilding from the ground up. By building each new level upon a strong, unadulterated foundation, one's teshuvah will stand for eternity.

Points to Ponder:

- *Regret is an essential component of complete teshuvah.*
- *Even if one abandons a sin "from now on," the sin he fails to regret acts as a barrier between himself and God.*

---

2. *Bamidbar* 15:31.

3. *Sifri, Bamidbar* 15:31.

4. *Rashi*, ad loc.

Never Again

> *"Oh, no! There's a cop coming behind me!" Yossi thought to himself. A quick glance at the speedometer — 85 miles per hour — told him that he could never talk his way out of this one.*
>
> *"License and registration, sir," the officer said as he approached Yossi's car. As Yossi handed him the documents, the officer said sternly, "I'm going to have to give you a ticket. Next time, watch your speed."*
>
> *"I'm sorry, officer," Yossi told the policeman. "Next time, I'll watch for speed traps," Yossi said to himself.*

Yossi's response reflects the spiritual approach of one who errs, admits his error, but makes no commitment to refrain from repeating it. For instance, someone who cheats in business may say, "I know it's not right, but it's a jungle out there. If I don't do it to them, they'll do it to me!" If he doesn't formulate a plan to stop his cheating, then his "I know it's not right" is ineffective in terms of teshuvah.

This phenomenon is reflected in the laws of immersion in a mikveh. For some forms of spiritual impurity, only the water of a mikveh can render the person pure. However, immersion will not be effective if the person holds a source of impurity; for instance, the carcass of an insect or a reptile, and brings it with him into the purifying water. He has to shed the impure object before he enters the water, or nothing can be achieved. Similarly, teshuvah will not work for someone still holding onto his sin.

Therefore, the second step in teshuvah, after regretting our sin, is to "forsake it," to abandon it and make a heartfelt commitment[1] to never again engage in that act.[2] This is not an "I'll try to do better" commitment. Rather, it is a heartfelt commitment so resolute that God Himself can testify to the sincerity of the person's intentions.[3]

What is God seeking when He looks into one's heart? He is looking for the person's firm resolution to shed his "evil ways" — the personality trait, situation, or mistaken belief that led him to do wrong.[4] If the person does not forsake the root of the sin, he is likely to relapse when faced with the challenge.[5] This means that a person who cheats in business because of his overpower-

---

1. See *Sifsei Chaim, Moadim*, Vol. 1, p. 237, s.v. *Es ikar,* who cites *Mabit, Beis Elokim*, Ch. 2, that the commitment is in his heart.

2. *Sifsei Chaim, Moadim*, Vol. 1, p. 236, s.v. *Amnam Rabbeinu Yonah.*

3. *Rambam, Hilchos Teshuvah* 2:2: "What constitutes teshuvah? That a sinner should abandon his sins and remove them from his thoughts, resolving in his heart never to commit them again ..."

4. *Shaarei Teshuvah, Shaar* 1:11.

5. *Matnas Chelko*, on *Shaarei Teshuvah*, p. 27.

ing love of money must resolve firmly to reform that trait. Otherwise, a resolution to refrain from cheating is doomed to failure.[6]

This step may require a serious reassessment of one's priorities and basic assumptions. In the opening story, as long as Yossi's self-image remains unchanged, he will not change his driving habits. Thus, Yossi has to make a firm commitment to stop driving like the thrill-seeking, aggressive young man that he is, and instead, resolve to keep a safe distance behind cars.

Forsaking a sin means revising our self-image, and that is why this is the most difficult part of any teshuvah.[7] Nevertheless, this is the heart of the power of teshuvah. We become better people: people energized by the incomparable joy of having worked hard at teshuvah, spawning blessings and clearing a path between ourselves and our Creator.

Points to Ponder:

- *In teshuvah, after regret, the second step is to forsake the sin.*
- *This means committing oneself to never repeating the sin.*
- *Forsaking a sin necessitates revising one's self-image, where the sin is rooted.*
- *Sincerely forsaking a sin makes one into a new person.*

---

6. *Sanhedrin* 25a, *Rashi*, s.v. *V'yachzir aveidah;* 25b, s.v. *D'afilu l'nachri.* See Day 34: Technique 1: Treat Causes, Not Symptoms.
7. See *Sifsei Chaim, Moadim*, Vol. 1, p. 242, s.v. *Zehu kushi,* citing Rabbi Yisroel Salanter.

Defining "Never"

At age 55, Josh realized that, despite having a wife, six children, 10 grandchildren, numerous neighbors and business associates, he was alone. His abrasive nature had gradually driven everyone away. He was tolerated, but not valued and sought out.

"It's now or never," he thought. "I've got to change!" His daughter and her family were coming for dinner that night, and he was determined to be a kinder and gentler Daddy.

A few hours later, the family sat around the table talking. Josh's wife, daughter and son-in-law were all enjoying Josh's new, softer manner. It was going just as Josh had hoped until his daughter began discussing her choice of yeshivah for her little boy.

"Are you out of your mind?" Josh exploded. "That place is falling apart! How can you be so blind?" As the words tumbled out of his mouth, he saw his family subtly recoil. The invisible

*wall between him and them snapped into place. It was hope-
less.*

Anyone who has ever taken it upon himself to change a negative trait understands what is meant by "two steps forward,
one step back." Does that mean that our resolution is not real and
our teshuvah is not accepted? How many of us could pass the litmus test "that God Himself would be able to testify to the sincerity
of our commitment to abandon their sin"?[1]

In reality, God's testimony does not mean that He looks into
the future and confirms that the person will never sin again.[2]
Rather, He establishes whether, at the time we commit ourselves to abandoning the sin, we have resolved with all our
heart to never again return to it. Making that sincere commitment elevates us to a new spiritual level, and God — Who knows
the hidden depths of our hearts — can testify that at our new,
elevated state, we will never return to the sin.

In the classic mode of teshuvah, the step of abandoning the
sin comes after the first step of sincere regret. That is because
regret motivates us to commit ourselves to never repeating the
sin.

There are situations, however, in which the first step must
be to forsake the negative traits and actions that constitute our

---

1. *Rambam, Hilchos Teshuvah* 2:2.
2. *Lechem Mishneh* on *Rambam, Hilchos Teshuvah* 2:2; *Sifsei Chaim, Moadim*, Vol. 1,
p. 235, s.v. *HaRambam madgish*; ibid., p. 241, s.v. *HaMabit: Takanas HaShavim*,
Siman 9, footnote 5.

sins. That occurs when we are so comfortably attached to our negative habits and traits that we see nothing to regret.[3]

For instance, someone who loves to gossip may often state, "I'd better cut out this *lashon hara*," and yet, he maintains his delight in hearing and passing on the latest gossip. For that person, abandoning the sin must come first. He must keep himself away from *lashon hara*-provoking situations and begin to de-acclimate himself to the sin before a new sensitivity and true regret can emerge.

For this individual, bad traits and habits are rooted like crabgrass in his heart. They will continue to spread, sprout, and re-grow unless they are uprooted.[4] There is work to be done, and God is waiting with "open arms."

Points to Ponder:

- *The sincerity of one's resolve to change is judged according to his feelings at the time.*

- *Someone who is habitually attached to a certain sin may be desensitized to it and fail to feel regret.*

- *In such a case, forsaking the sin is the proper first step to real change. Regret develops from there.*

---

3. *Shaarei Teshuvah, Shaar* 1:11.

4. See *Yeshaya* 55:7.

Viduy /
Verbal Confession

Avraham drove away from his house with a knot of anger gnawing inside him. He and his wife had argued. It was her fault. She was too demanding.

As he turned onto the highway, a thought flickered in his mind. "It was my fault ... I never really listened to what she was saying ... I have to fix that ... . Oh boy, a traffic jam ... Look at the time ... Why is that guy changing lanes? Maybe there's road-work ahead .... She's probably all upset .... I really better fix things ... What's with all this traffic?"

Our minds are a nonstop monologue encompassing thoughts as sublime as remorse and self-improvement, and as mundane as the traffic flow. Thoughts flit through our consciousness helter-skelter, each roosting only until another comes to displace it. Therefore, teshuvah must manifest itself in something more than thought.

Viduy,[1] in which we verbally[2] confess our sins to God,[3] is so important that it is counted as one of the 613 commandments[4]. In addition, verbal expression intensifies the internal impact of our words.[5] Thus, it is logical, at the critical crossroads between sin and repentance, to decisively propel ourselves in the right direction with the power of the spoken word.

Viduy transfers teshuvah from the realm of amorphous thought into reality. It enhances the feeling of conversing with a second party. One must view himself as if he is actually standing before Hashem acknowledging that by sinning he has rebelled against the King and that he is asking forgiveness.[6] In this way, he can more keenly sense that God is aware of his every deed, and that he is accountable before God for everything he does.

Yet, *Viduy* is not just an action that one does for himself to concretize his feelings of regret. V*iduy* is the act of conversing before a loving God in which one acknowledges that he has

---

1. *Bamidbar* 5:7. "And they shall confess their sin which they committed." See *Shaarei Teshuvah, Shaar* 1:40.

2. See *She'eilos U'Teshuvos, Teshuvos V'Hanhagos,* Vol. 4, *Siman* 148, p. 137, s.v. *Bakashah.*

3. See *Shaarei Teshuvah, Shaar* 1:40, and *Beis Elokim, Shaar HaTeshuvah,* Ch. 3, s.v. *V'hinei ha'vidu.*

4. *Bamidbar* 5:7.

5. *Sifsei Chaim, Bereishis,* p. 181.

6. *Sefer HaChinuch,* Mitzvah 364.

sinned thereby creating a divide between himself and God. The result of the *Viduy* is to remove the sin so that he can come close to the Almighty."[7] This explains why *Viduy* on Yom Kippur is said as part of *tefillah*, which is the ultimate expression of man's close relationship with God.[8]

> *Rabbi Shimon Schwab was once waiting for a streetcar in Baltimore. A woman emerged from a nearby church and approached him. "Rabbi Schwab, you're probably surprised to see me coming from there," she said.*
>
> *Rabbi Schwab assured her that he was rarely surprised by anything he saw.*
>
> *"Actually, I'm Jewish," she continued. "I went to a priest to unburden myself. I don't see him, he doesn't see me, and he asks no questions."*
>
> *"We Jews have confession." Rabbi Schwab informed her. "We say it everyday. It's called Viduy. In fact, on Yom Kippur we say Viduy nine times."*
>
> *Rabbi Schwab reminded her that our loving God is always listening and is always available. "Every person is free at any time throughout the year, either before he goes to bed or whenever, to confess to God."*

Despite the power of *Viduy*, it cannot stand alone as teshuvah. Without the prerequisites of regret and of forsaking the

---

7. Ibid.
8. *Sichos R' Shimshon Dovid Pincus, Elul, Yamim Noraim*, p. 371.

sin,[9] a verbal confession is just lip service, comparable to a humiliated child's forced "I'm sorry," voiced to please his parents and end the episode.[10]

We cannot place a roof upon a house that has no framework. Yet, a house without a roof is useless. In teshuvah, regret and forsaking the sin form the framework. If they are not topped by *Viduy,* they will not completely serve their function. On the other hand, *Viduy* alone is like a roof plopped down upon a house that is supposed to be there, but isn't. Only when the first two steps are in place does *Viduy* establish our teshuvah, eradicating past sins and making way for fresh progress.

Points to Ponder:

- *Verbally stating one's feelings makes them more concrete and enhances their impact.*

- *Without Viduy, teshuvah is incomplete. However, verbal confession, without first feeling regret and forsaking one's sin, is empty.*

---

9. These three components suffice for sins between man and Hashem. For sins between man and his fellow man. See *Chinuch*, mitzvah 364.
10. See *Chofetz Chaim on the Torah, Parashas Bechukosai* 26:40-41, p. 182. See also *Ohr HaChaim, Chizkuni,* and *Aderes Eliyahu,* ibid.

Laws of Verbal Confession

*W*hen a person is ready to embark on the "action" portion of teshuvah, the part that turns it from a thought and a feeling into a reality, he is once again in need of precise instructions. Just as teshuvah itself cannot be approached in a haphazard way if it is to accomplish its miraculous effect, likewise, *Viduy* must be recited according to specific guidelines so that it can successfully fufill its essential role.

The first ingredient in *Viduy* is the emotion entailed. Reciting a list of sins in a rote manner will not afford what *Viduy* is capable of accomplishing.[1] Obviously, we are not telling God something He doesn't know. Rather, we "come clean" to elicit God's help in healing our deficiency, and to move forward.

---

1. *Sforno* on *Devarim* 30:8.

A synopsis of the laws of Viduy follows:

- The words of the *Viduy* said on Yom Kippur are specified in the Machzor. For *Viduy* said throughout the year, there is no specific wording.[2] Rather, we should reach into ourselves to find a sense of true humility, and confess to God with complete concentration, in a settled, calm state of mind.
- Although halachah does not demand that we specify each sin,[3] it is preferable to do so.[4]
- Verbal confession is not a public act, as we must acknowledge our misdeeds to God privately. It is considered disrespectful to Hashem for a person to publicize the ways in which he has disobeyed Him.[5]
- *Viduy* should be recited standing,[6] in a bowed posture similar to that used during the *Modim* prayer of *Shemoneh Esrei*.[7] One might not be considered to be standing if he is leaning on something — table, chair, wall, etc. — so fully

---

2. This does not have to be said in Hebrew. See *Koveitz Halachos* on *Yamim Noraim, Mitzvas Teshuvah, Viduy,* that the exact words of *Viduy* that one must recite is unclear. See also *Midrash Shocher Tov,* Chapter 45, s.v. *Rachash; Rosh, Moed Katan,* Chapter 3, *Siman* 76; *Minchas Chinuch,* Mitzvah 364:1,3; *Sheilos U'Teshuvos Lev Chaim,* Vol. 1, *Siman* 10; and *Derech Sicha,* Vol. 1, p. 615, s.v. *Shema hirhur.*

3. See *Halichos Shlomo, Moadim,* Chapter 4, *Se'if* 2 that for a sin that one has transgressed many times, he should say, "The specific sin that I transgressed many times."

4. *Siman* 607, *Se'if* 2.

5. See *Aruch HaShulchan, Siman* 602, *Se'if* 13; *Orach Chaim, Siman* 607, *Se'if* 2.

6. *Orach Chaim,* 607:3.

7. *Magen Avraham,* 607:4.

that, if the support were to be unexpectedly removed, he would fall.[8] In that case, his *Viduy* might not be valid.[9]

- We lightly strike our chest over our heart with our fist, as if to say, "You [the heart] have led me to sin."[10]
- If someone has already confessed a sin properly, for instance, on the previous Yom Kippur, and he has not since repeated it, he need not mention it again.[11] However, there is merit in re-confessing a sin.[12] In doing so, we fulfill the verse, "And my sin is ever before me,"[13] (due to regret, not repetition of the sin).

The halachos of *Viduy* serve to amplify the humility and sincerity integral to teshuvah. However, within this tone of seriousness is a spark of joy.

> *Arriving at a certain town before Yom Kippur, the Baal Shem Tov asked the residents how the shliach tzibbur conducts himself when reciting Viduy. They told him that he had an unusual custom of singing.*
>
> *The Baal Shem at once called for this man and asked him the meaning of his custom. The man answered with a parable,*

---

8. Ibid.

9. *Pri Megadim, Aishel Avraham* 4. See *Kaf Hachaim, Siman* 607, *Os* 23. That a sick or elderly person may lean.

10. *Magen Avraham Siman* 607, *Se'if Katan* 4, citing the *Midrash Rabbah, Koheles* 7.

11. *Shulchan Aruch, Orach Chaim*, 607:4.

12. *Magen Avraham*, 607:6, from *Yoma* 86a.

13. *Tehillim* 51:5.

"If the lowliest of a king's servants, whose task is to rake away the filth from the gutters of the royal courtyard, loves his king, then as he works he sings with joy out of the sheer pleasure he derives from making the king happy!"

"If this is what you have in mind while you are saying the Viduy," said the Baal Shem Tov, "then I wish that my lot were at one with yours!"[14]

What this *shaliach tzibbur* felt, and what every sincere penitent discovers, is that *Viduy* is indeed conducive to joy.

Joy, derived from cleansing away the sins, is the emotion a person experiences when he comes closer to God. He feels uplifted, sanctified, and enriched. This fills his heart with a boundless joy so profound that it allows God's "light" to enter our hearts unimpeded.[15]

Points to Ponder:

- *Saying Viduy properly requires adherence to specific rules.*

- *A sincere, properly recited confession turns our teshuvah into something concrete and effective.*

---

14. Adapted from *A Treasury of Chassidic Tales*, Rabbi S.Y. Zevin, ArtScroll, p. 118.
15. Adapted from *With Hearts Full of Faith,* Rabbi Mattisyahu Salomon and Rabbi Yaakov Yosef Reinman, ArtScroll / Mesorah p. 84.

The Final Hurdle

*H*ow does one know that his teshuvah is really, certainly, and totally complete? How can one be sure that there isn't one more step that he needs to take before our sin can be considered erased?

The Talmud[1] pondered this question, asking, "What are the circumstances that define one who has repented completely?" In response, the criteria for complete teshuvah is: "The person has completely repented when an opportunity for the sin he committed in the past[2] comes his way a first time and a second time, and on both occasions,[3] he overcomes his evil inclination."[4]

These tests must actually replicate in every significant way

---

1. *Yoma* 86b.

2. *Rashi*, ibid., s.v. *She'ba davar*.

3. See ibid., *Anaf Yosef; Ben Yehoyada*. Of course he should not put himself into a situation where he will be tempted to sin. Rather, the intent is that his repentance should be so sincere that if the opportunity to sin would arise again, he would not succumb.

4. *Maharsha*, ibid., s.v. *V'nitzol heimena*. See *Tzidkas HaTzaddik, Os* 99.

the circumstances under which the person first committed the sin. This is the real test, because the identical circumstances are most likely to evoke an identical response.[5] The person's motives for refraining from the sin must be sincere, and not from lack of strength.[6]

Turning away from the sin is a tangible step that takes teshuvah out of the nebulous realms of the heart and mind and makes it a reality. As long as our thoughts do not translate into action, there is something lacking in our thoughts.[7]

Yet, we must wonder: would it not seem that, in orchestrating a return to the same circumstances that led to a person's fall, God is simply clearing the path to further sin? If a child falls off his bike every time he takes a certain route, would a loving parent allow him to take that route twice more, just to see if he manages to avoid injury?

The answer[8] is that God is definitively not abandoning the person to his sins but rather, He is enabling him to confront them.[9] A "*baal teshuvah*" should not consider himself distant from the level of the righteous because of the sins and transgressions that he committed. He is beloved and desirable before the Creator. Furthermore, he has a great reward, for he has

5. *Rashi* ibid., s.v. *B'osa*. See ibid., *Ran, Shiltei HaGiborim* for an additional explanation.

6. *Rambam, Hilchos Teshuvah* 2:1.

7. *Ohr Gedalyahu, Bereishis*, p. 51 citing *Noam Elimelech*.

8. *Rambam, Hilchos Teshuvah* 7:4.

9. *Tzidkas HaTzaddik, Os* 73.

tasted sin and yet, separated himself from it, conquering his evil inclination.

In fact, if one finds himself confronted with the identical situation that spurred his previous error, he should realize that he is standing in that spot because of God's grace. This is a sign of amazing heavenly help, as Hashem has arranged this situation only to give him the opportunity to overcome his evil inclination this time, and to be considered to have done complete teshuvah.[10]

If this act of twice rejecting the sin under the same circumstances is the litmus test for complete teshuvah, what happens to someone whose sin cannot be replicated exactly? For instance, what if a man cheated in business when his business was in dire straits, but now it is prospering? Can such a person ever achieve complete *teshuvah?*

In the case where new circumstances have eliminated the possibility to re-encounter the exact same sin, the path to complete teshuvah is to make a concerted effort to increase one's *yiras Shamayim*[11] each day. By doing so, one builds himself into a person who indeed would have withstood the test, had it arisen. The measure of one's spiritual progress is apparent to God, who therefore considers such a person a *"baal teshuvah."*

---

10. *Matnas Chelko*, on *Shaarei Teshuvah*, p. 74.
11. See Day 19: Strategy 3: "Increase Yiras Shamayim."

Points to Ponder:

- *A person is considered to have done complete teshuvah when he has twice withstood circumstances identical to those that led to his sin.*

- *God places the person in identical circumstances not to trip him, but to provide an opportunity to pass his test.*

- *If the same circumstances cannot occur, the person should instead work on his own spiritual growth to establish the completion of his teshuvah.*

Repair Character Flaws

"I can't help it. That's just the way I am." Everyone has either said these words, heard them, or both. Nevertheless, Rav Avraham Pam would often paraphrase the Rambam's rebuttal of this justification with the words, "It's not your nature; it's your choice." [1]

Negative character traits, which express themselves through the nature of our desires, can be tamed and held under tight control, but they are almost never benign. These desires cause a person to conceive distorted thoughts, which in turn give birth to mistaken beliefs and actions. [2] Therefore, mistakes made in our decision-making process emanate from the root of this process:

---

1. *Rambam, Hilchos Teshuvah* 5:1.
2. *Michtav MeEliyahu*, Vol. 1, p. 121.

our desires, which are shaped by our character.[3] A person's bad character traits, such as haughtiness and self-centeredness, will cause him to slant and distort the Torah's truth.[4]

The first step in repairing negative traits[5] is to identify them, take responsibility for them, and acknowledge the harm they do to us and to others.

> *A criminal court judge demanded that defendants of particularly heinous crimes write a 2,000-word essay about how their crime affected themselves and others, and how they could avoid such episodes in the future. None of the essays — including those of people who killed others through drunken driving, or murdered innocents in the course of petty robberies — included one word of remorse. Rather, the defendants wrote extensive hard-luck narratives blaming their crime on everyone but themselves.[6]*

In today's guilt-free culture, reforming bad character presents a major challenge. The undeniable reality, however, is that even if a person paints himself as an innocent victim of circum-

---

3. See *Sifsei Chaim, Moadim,* Vol. 1, p. 185.

4. *Bereishis Rabbah* 8:8, *Shaarei Kedushah,* Part 1, *Shaar* 2. See *Rambam, Hilchos Teshuvah* 2:2.

5. *Rambam, Hilchos Teshuvah* 7:3: "A person should not think that repentance is necessary only for those sins such as lewdness, robbery, or theft. He must repent of anger, hatred, envy, frivolity, the pursuit of money and honor, the pursuit of gluttony, and the like. He must repent of all of these."

6. Aish.com Sept. 14, 2009. The Crime I Didn't Commit by Sara Yoheved Rigler.

stance, nothing will change for him until he accepts responsibility for his behavior.

Changing a *middah* is widely acknowledged as one of the most difficult tasks a person can undertake.[7] The secret to success is to keep trying. The person who persists will find that one day, a challenge arises and his reaction is far different from what it would have previously been. Wonder of wonders, he has changed for the better.

Points to Ponder:

- *A person's character traits determine his behavior.*
- *Positive traits are the foundation of all mitzvos.*
- *Although changing a character trait is extremely difficult, it can be done.*

---

7. *Ohr Yisrael, Os* 30.

Middos Make the Man

The Rambam and a philosopher differed as to whether animal behavior arises from instinct or from training. The philosopher proposed that properly trained, an animal could emulate human behavior. To prove his point, he taught cats to stand erect, balance trays, and serve as waiters. He then held a banquet, using tuxedo-clad cats as the waiters. The Rambam had no need to utter one word to support his own argument. He merely released several mice and the cats, forgetting their training, let the trays and dishes crash to the ground as they scurried about on all fours to catch the mice.[1]

One way a person differs from an animal is his ability to perfect his *middos* and thereby overcome his baser instincts. A person who learns Torah without working to perfect his *middos* will, like the trained cat, be able to put on a show of propriety for some time, but only as long as no "mice" appear on the scene.[2]

---

1. Cited in *Ohr Yechezkel, Darkei HaAvodah*, p. 99, s.v. *V'hizkarnu*.
2. Aish.com, *Outlooks and Insights*, by Rabbi Zev Leff, September 29, 2003.

The Mishnah teaches, "Where there is no *derech eretz*, there is no Torah."[3] *Middos* are both the foundation and the result of Torah learning. Without Torah, the ultimate perfection of *middos* is impossible. Yet without *middos,* we cannot even begin to acquire Torah.Clearly it is well worth a person's effort to take an inventory of his personality traits, asking himself, "How do I react to frustration? How do I respond when asked for help? Do I lose my temper often? Why Am I on the outs with many people? Do I forgive others? Do I seek forgiveness when I'm wrong? *Am I ever wrong?*"

These are the necessary steps to becoming the individuals we are meant to be and the nation we are meant to be. By undertaking these steps, we can feel confident that soon, we will live in the world as it's meant to be: a world of peace, happiness, and blessing.

Points to Ponder:

- *Middos are needed for Torah to have a lasting impact on an individual.*

- *Middos are essential for passing Torah values to the next generation.*

- *Developing one's middos is essential to teshuvah, and thus, to redemption.*

---

3. *Avos* 3:22.

Asking Forgiveness

Shmuel's brother teased him and Shmuel hit him. The brother's nose started to bleed and he began crying hysterically. Their mother quickly arrived on the scene.

"I'm sorry, Mommy!" Shmuel cried out urgently, hoping to avoid punishment for his deed.

"Don't say you're sorry to me," his mother instructed. "Say it to your brother!"

If Shmuel refused to apologize to his brother, claiming that his provocation warranted his reaction, how likely would his mother be to accept his apology? When a person insults or damages another, the place to begin making amends is with the victim.

This is the guiding concept for the atonement we acquire on Yom Kippur for sins between ourselves and others. The Torah[1] promises that, "On this day, He shall provide atonement for you to cleanse you. From all your sins before Hashem shall you be

---

1. *Vayikra* 16:30.

cleansed."[2] Yom Kippur atones for sins between man and God.[3] For sins against our fellow man, the sinner must first seek to appease his victim and obtain his forgiveness[4] before he says *Viduy* for the sin.[5]

Teshuvah for acts against others can be achieved only in this fashion, whether the harm was physical, verbal, emotional, or financial, and whether it was committed in the person's presence or behind his back. For instance, if Reuven spoke *lashon hara* about Shimon, who thereby lost a job promotion, Reuven must approach Shimon directly, admit what he did, and ask for forgiveness.[6]

If Shimon is unaware of what was said about him, Reuven must tell him.[7] If the information will cause Shimon embarrassment or pain, or result in an argument,[8] between Reuven and Shimon, then Reuven need not tell him the *lashon hara* that was spoken.[9] A general request for forgiveness will suffice because there is no benefit in hurting Shimon further by repeating the negative words spoken about him.[10]

---

2. See *Yoma* 87a.

3. *Mishnah, Yoma* 8:9.

4. See *Birkei Yosef* 606:1 and *Hirurei Teshuvah* (Rav M. Gifter), p. 121.

5. *Shaarei Teshuvah* 1:16.

6. Quoted by *Chofetz Chaim, Lashon Hara* 4:12.

7. *Chofetz Chaim*, ibid.

8. *Kuntres Bein Adam L'Chaveiro, Siman* 16, cited in *Ashrei HaIsh*, Vol. 3, Harav Elyashiv, p. 127.

9. *Mishnah Berurah* 606:3.

10. Rav Yisroel Salanter, quoted by Rav Dessler and published in *Moadim u'Zemanim*

If Shimon had suffered no harm from the *lashon hara*, Reuven would not have to ask Shimon's forgiveness at all. He would be required, however, to repent for his sin and ask forgiveness directly from God.[11]

If someone requests forgiveness from many people as a group, but he knows that he transgressed against one person in particular, he does not fulfill his obligation.[12]

Asking for forgiveness is often an unpleasant task that requires a major act of contrition. No one likes to admit to himself, much less to the victim of his wrongdoing, that he has done something dishonest, insensitive or unkind. Because people naturally try to avoid painful or embarrassing encounters, they tend to delay asking for forgiveness for as long as possible.

On the other side of the equation is the victim, who has suffered at the hands of the wrongdoer. He forgives by letting go of his grievance against the wrongdoer and saying the words "I forgive you."[13] Many people find this difficult to do, fearing that forgiving somehow hands the wrongdoer a victory.

There are situations in which we have been victimized and humiliated. We are filled with righteous indignation against the

---

1:54. See *She'eilos U'Teshuvos Az Nidberu* 7:66, who rules in accordance with this view. In his opinion, as long as Shimon is unaware that *lashon hara* was spoken about him, there is absolutely no requirement to inform him of what was said. See also *Derech Sichah*, Vol. 1, p. 623.

11. *Sha'arei Teshuvah* 207, quoted by *Chofetz Chaim, Lashon Hara* 4:12.

12. *Mishnah Berurah* 606:3.

13. See *Rabbeinu Bachya*, *Bereishis* 50:17.

sinner and we know with absolute clarity that he is wrong and we are right, in the same way that a person who sins is wrong, and God is right. In such situations, saying "I forgive you" is a *segulah* that will unlock heaven's mercy in our favor."[14] For this reason, repentance for sins against others is the perfect preparation for our repentance for sins against God.

Points to Ponder:

- *For sins against our fellow man, we must first make amends before we seek God's forgiveness.*

- *One benefits greatly by forgiving another who apologizes sincerely.*

- *The humility engendered by making amends with our fellow man prepares one for seeking amends with Hashem.*

---

14. *Tomer Devorah* end of Ch. 1.

Asking Forgiveness: The Laws

*W*e overcome our own resistance, admit our guilt, and bring ourselves to the difficult decision to ask forgiveness of another person. In any situation in which we have wronged another person, leaving the wound unhealed can be devastating to our lives in this world and the Next World. With so much invested in making things right, with a dose of humility and the Torah's wise direction, we can rely on the Torah's guidelines to ensure that we achieve the forgiveness we are seeking, both from our fellow and from Hashem. In this way, we can release both ourselves and those we have wronged from the terrible burden of hurt and anger, and pave the path to blessings through forgiveness.

A synopsis of the relevant laws follows:

Who to Approach

- Even if we upset someone only with words, we are still obligated to make amends.[1]
- We should ask another person for forgiveness even if the person's grievance seems unjustified.[2]
- If we are not sure whether we have harmed another person, we must ask forgiveness, stating that we are unsure if harm was done.[3]
- Every person must ask family members (i.e. parents, spouse) and rebbeim for forgiveness because of the likelihood of having caused them pain or embarrassment.[4]
- Even if we know that the other person has already forgiven us, we should still approach him and ask forgiveness because this builds our humility, which is essential to teshuvah.[5]

Persistence

- If we are not forgiven initially, we should try a second and a third time.[6] These can all be during one interaction.[7]

---

1. *Siman* 606, *Se'if* 1.
2. *Mekor Chaim, Siman* 606, *Se'if* 1; *Sfas Emes* on *Yoma* 87b, s.v. *Ikpid*. See *Koveitz Halachos* on Yamim Noraim, *Mitzvas Teshuvah, Viduy.*
3. *Kuntras Bein Adam L'Chaveiro, Siman* 51, cited in *Ashrei HaIsh*, Vol. 3, Harav Elyashiv, p. 127. See also *Aruch HaShulchan, Siman* 606, *Se'if* 4.
4. *Ben Ish Chai, Parashas Vayeilach*, Os 6. See also *Koveitz Halachos* on Yamim Noraim, *Mitzvas Teshuvah, Viduy;* See also *Aruch HaShulchan Siman* 606, *Se'if* 4.
5. *Ashrei Ha'Ish*, Vol. 3, Harav Elyashiv, p. 127; See *Koveitz Halachos* on Yamim Noraim, *Pi'us Chaveiro.*
6. *Siman* 606, *Se'if* 1.
7. *Mekor Chaim, Siman* 606, *Se'if* 1, s.v. *Yachzor v'yeileich.*

- The first time one goes to ask forgiveness, he can go alone to appease the other.[8] If he is not successful, then he should bring three men (even minors[9]) each time he goes to seek forgiveness. They can be the same or different men.[10]
- If the person still refuses forgiveness after three attempts, we need not persist.[11]

An Intermediary

- It is generally better to seek forgiveness in person (or by phone) from someone we have wronged. A written apology (letter) does not have the status of asking in person. The reason is that a person has to humble himself to ask personally, as this is part of the forgiveness process.[12]
- If it is too difficult logistically to personally seek forgiveness or if we believe that the person will be more receptive to an intermediary, we can use an intermediary.[13]
- If a person cannot reach the person or send an intermediary before Yom Kippur, he should commit himself to seek forgiveness as soon as he is able.[14]

---

8. *Koveitz Halachos* on Yamim Noraim, *Pi'us Chaveiro*. See *Beur Halacha, Siman* 606, Se'if 1 who discusses this issue. The prevalent custom is to go ask alone possibly because the aggrieved person usually forgives at that time.

9. *Koveitz Halachos* on Yamim Noraim, *Pi'us Chaveiro.*

10. *Kaf HaChaim, Siman* 606, *Se'if Katan* 17.

11. *Orach Chaim, Siman* 606, *Se'if* 1. See *Rama,* Ad loc; *Mishneh Berurah* Ad loc *Se'if Katan* 6.

12. *Koveitz Halachos* on Yamim Noraim, *Pi'us Chaveiro.*

13. *Siman* 606, *Mishneh Berurah, Se'if Katan* 2.

14. *Yapheh L'Laiv,* Vol. 6, *Os* 2.

Specific Situations

- If a person steals from someone, even if he has returned the item and received forgiveness, he should still confess the sin on Yom Kippur, because his sin was also against God.[15]
- If one embarrasses someone in public, he must ask forgiveness in public (not necessarily before those who heard the embarrassing comment).[16]

Forgiveness From a Minor

- If we harm a minor — a boy under the age of 13 or a girl under 12 — the custom is to ask for forgiveness even though, according to Jewish law, the child's forgiveness is ineffective. When the child reaches maturity, we are obligated to ask for forgiveness again.[17]

With these guidelines, we can assure ourselves that we have done our part in finding anyone from whom we need forgiveness, and that we have tried as hard as Hashem expects us to try to make amends. We can then turn ourselves toward Heaven and ask Hashem to forgive us, as well.

---

15. *Siman* 607, *Mishneh Berurah*, *Se'if Katan* 13; *Pri Megadim*, *Mishbetzos Zahav*, ibid, *Se'if Katan* 1.

16. *Mekor Chaim*, *Siman* 606, *Se'if* 1, s.v. *B'zahu*. In all cases, it is sufficient in front of 10 people.

17. *Ashrei HaIsh*, Vol. 3, Harav Elyashiv, p. 126; *Kovetz Halachos* on Yamim Noraim *Pi'us Chaveiro*.

Points to Ponder:

- *Anyone we have wronged, including family members, teachers, students, and even minors, should be asked for forgiveness.*

- *We can approach the person we have wronged on our own, or bring three people with us.*

- *We are required to try three times to attain the other person's forgiveness. These can all be during the same interaction.*

Acknowledgments

As I sat down to write the acknowledgments to this book, it occurred to me that every day we recite the same Modim in *Shemoneh Esrei* thanking Hashem even though each additional day we are graced with more life. The reason is that although the words of Modim are the same, the thought and feelings behind the words do indeed grow each day. Therefore, I will repeat the acknowledgments that were included in the previous books.

The first place in the Torah where the Hebrew word for "thanks" appears is when Leah gave birth to her fourth son, Yehudah. She said, "This time I will thank Hashem." Rashi comments that Leah felt grateful to Hashem for each of her children. However, when she gave birth to Yehudah, she recognized and admitted to Hashem that she had been granted sons beyond her fair share. True thanksgiving occurs when people feel they have been given more than they deserve.

To have had the *zechus* (merit) to author the **Praying With Fire** series (**Praying With Fire 1 and 2**) and **Yearning With Fire** was more than I ever dreamed. To have even imagined that I would have the opportunity to author **The Power of Teshuvah** is truly beyond contemplation. Once again I thank Hashem for giving me yet another opportunity. *All* this happened only due to great *siyata d'Shmaya*, Heavenly Help.

In the *Modim* blessing of *Shemoneh Esrei*, we exclaim: "We shall thank You and relate Your praise — **for our lives,** which are committed to Your power, and for our souls ... that are entrusted to You ..." We normally take our existence for granted. Thus, with these words we admit to Hashem that every moment of our lives is a gift that He has granted us.

I thank **HaKadosh Baruch Hu** for continuing to grant me life with its numerous gifts. These include providing me with health, the means, the ideas, the people from whom I have learned, and the time necessary to undertake this endeavor along with countless other remarkable details too numerous to mention.

Hodaah

The Hebrew word for thanksgiving is *hodaah*. This word also means "to admit." Rav Hutner comments that when one person gives thanks to another he is really admitting that he needed the other person.

The Gemara teaches us the extent of our requirement to show *hakaras hatov* by informing us that one should not throw a rock into a pit of water from which he draws. At first glance, the duty to thank the water appears odd. Water is an inanimate object, it has no feelings, nor did it intend to help us.

Rav Dessler explains *Chazal's* profound lesson, that our need to show thanks is not because the giver bothered or was inconvenienced on our behalf, or that he intended to perform a service for us. Our requirement to express thanks is solely because we were the recipient of good that should cause our hearts to swell with positive feelings toward the giver. This should compel us to reciprocate and give back even more than what we received, the least of which is to first express our sincere heartfelt thanks.

Many heartfelt thanks are in order to those who were instrumental in the writing and completion of **The Power of Teshuvah**.

I thank **HaRav Mattisyahu Salomon,** *shlit"a, Mashgiach* of the Lakewood Yeshivah, Beis Medrash Govoha for allowing me to include a foreword for this book.

Much thanks to **Rabbi Meir Zlotowitz** and **Rabbi Nosson Scherman** of ArtScroll, who graciously gave me the opportunity to write **The Power of Teshuvah**. We are all indebted to them for having provided all members of Klal Yisrael with the opportunity to learn about so many vital topics affecting our spirituality.

Thanks to **Mendy Herzberg** for coordinating all the aspects of the project at ArtScroll until its completion. Thanks to **Gedaliah Zlotowitz** for his wisdom. Thanks to **Eli Kroen** for his expert input. His exceptional eye and flare for perfection is evident in the design of the all-important book cover.

Thanks to **Mrs. Estie Dicker** and **Mrs. Toby Goldzweig** for their typing expertise. Thanks to **Rabbi Sheah Brander,** ArtScroll's master craftsman, whose indelible fingerprint is on every page. Thanks to **Mrs. Reizy Ganz** and **Shloime Brander** for skillfully paginating each page and for its aesthetics. Thank you to **Mrs. Faygie Weinbaum** for proofreading in her usual meticulous way.

Mrs. Mindy Stern's devoted attention to every word and nuance in this book has added immeasurably to its quality. A master of her craft, her contributions are highly valued and deeply appreciated.

Great thanks to **Mrs. Judi Dick** of ArtScroll who once again selflessly gave of her editing talents, experience, and dedication in bringing this work to its completion. The largesse of her dedication, selflessness, and expertise is surpassed only by her heart.

Once again, I offer a special note of thanks to the principal editor of the book, **Mrs. Chana Nestlebaum** — not just from myself, but on behalf of the readers of this book who will benefit most from her words of passion, expertise in editing, and ability to "keep it flowing." May Hashem shower her with great merit for all she has done.

I would also like to thank **Rabbi Ezra Bloch** of Lakewood, New Jersey, for reviewing the manuscript and the many footnotes. I pray that the footnotes will enable the scholar to take a more enlightening approach in understanding this book. Much thanks to my oldest son, **Rabbi Daniel Osher Kleinman,** who reviewed the important halachos of *Viduy*.

I am deeply grateful to **Mrs. Sharon First** who has served the

V'Ani Tefillah Foundation with true dedication and zeal for the last few years. Under pressure and on short notice, she has been able to accomplish the task of a team of others. She has played a key role in spreading the Foundation's message of the need and the ability to come closer to Hashem. Shuls, schools, and communities not only nationwide, but across the globe, have gained from her efforts. May Hashem give her the abilities to continue to help Klal Yisrael grow in spirituality and to hasten the Geulah.

Special thanks to **Mrs. Chana Finkelstein** of Masterpiece Design for the concept of the book cover. Mrs. Finkelstein, through her exceptional graphic artwork, has truly enhanced the work of the V'Ani Tefillah Foundation, and helped us communicate our message so successfully. Her beautiful eye-catching designs, her patience, and her devoted work under pressure are greatly appreciated.

Chazal teach that one's wife is called the "home." Special thanks to my wife **Bruria**, a true *eishes chayil,* for creating a home in which the learning and teaching of Torah and the doing of *chesed* is paramount. Because of her selfless support, I was able to disappear for hours on end in order to undertake the writing of this book. May Hashem bless her with great merit for all she does.

I apologize to anyone who assisted in this book in any way, whose name I have inadvertently omitted. To **all** who have assisted with **The Power of Teshuvah,** may Hashem shower you with the great merit that accrues to those who enlighten and uplift the public.

Finally, I thank you, the reader, for your desire to help Klal Yisrael return to Hashem. I pray that each day of learning about the power of teshuvah brings each of us a step closer to the day when our teshuvah along with the prayers, tears, and longings for the redemption will be answered by our loving Father in Heaven.

The V'Ani Tefillah Foundation

The V'Ani Tefillah Foundation's (VAT) mission is to increase awareness of the importance and power of tefillah, emunah and teshuvah and to provide education, inspiration and tools for "coming closer" to Hashem.

Since its inception in 2005, VAT has successfully put forth numerous tefillah and emunah programs and initiatives, which have had an impact on **millions of tefillos** around the world. Below is a list of some of the many programs available from the VAT:

BOOKS:
- *'PRAYING WITH FIRE 1' — A 5-MINUTE-LESSON-A-DAY FORMAT CONTAINS 89 DAILY LESSONS*
- *'PRAYING WITH FIRE 2' — A 5-MINUTE-LESSON-A-DAY FORMAT CONTAINS 118 DAILY LESSONS*
- *'YEARNING WITH FIRE' — A 5-MINUTE-LESSON-A-DAY FORMAT CONTAINS 89 DAILY LESSONS*
- *'THE POWER OF TESHUVAH' — A 5-MINUTE-LESSON-A-DAY FORMAT CONTAINS 40 DAILY LESSONS*

- **Impact: Inspiring over 100,000 Worldwide**
Over 100,000 people were inspired by the first volume of 'Praying With Fire', as of Elul, 5771.
PWF: Chapters Include:
- The Immeasurable Power of Tefillah • Achieving Personal Growth Through Tefillah • Gaining a Proper Understanding of Kavannah • 13 Practical Strategies to Achieve True Kavannah • Finding Answers to Unanswered Prayers
PWF 2: Chapters Include:
- Emunah & Tefillah: The Antidote to Fear and Terrorism • Emunah

& Bitachon: The Foundation of Prayer • 8 Practical Strategies To Strengthen Emunah and Bitachon • Building Your Relationship With Your Creater • 14 Practical Strategies To Getting Prayers Accepted • The Power of Praying For Others

YWF: Chapters Include:

• Longing for the Geulah • Creating a People United • Ending Jealousy and Hatred • V'ahavta L'rei'acha Kamocha • Revealing Hashem's Presence

ASERES YEMEI TESHUVAH INITIATIVES
5765 (2005), 5766 (2006), 5768 (2008), 5770 (2010):

• **Impact: Inspiring Hundreds of Thousands Worldwide**

In 5765\2005; 5766\2006, and 5768\2008 over **100,000 Booklets** (each time) with inspiring 10-day excerpts from **'Praying With Fire'** and **'Praying With Fire 2'** were distributed free each year to 250 cities in 10 countries around the world. By distributing these booklets, thousands each year gained a new appreciation of the power of each prayer to stir the Heavens and alter the fabric of their daily lives during the most important time of the year for tefillah.

In 5768\2008 over 100,000 Booklets with inspiring 10-day excerpts from **'Praying With Fire 2'** were distributed free to 250 cities in 10 countries around the world. In addition to the 'The Power of Praying For Others' booklet, a bookmark to be inserted in a siddur was distributed which gave people the opportunity to list names of those to daven for during Shemoneh Esrei.

The merit of praying for another Jew is so immense that the Gemara (Bava Kamma 92a) states that anyone who prays for mercy on behalf of his fellow when he himself is in need of that same thing, he is answered first. In fact, every individual who prays for members of the community—his prayers are a thousand times more valuable than if every individual had merely prayed for himself, says Michtav M'Eliyahu.

In 5770/2010 over 30,000 booklets with inspiring 10-day excerpts regarding hastening the redemption from **Yearning With Fire** were distributed free, around the world.

SHUL TEFILLAH INITIATIVE

• **Impact: Over 145 shuls in 34 communities have participated in the shul Tefillah Initiative.**

Now is the time for your shul to join the over 145 shuls in 34 communities who have already participated in the Shul Tefillah Initiative. The Shul Tefillah Initiative works with the whole shul together to strengthen collective tefillos in each shul. The Initiative entails learning the 89 five-minute lessons-a-day of Praying With Fire – Volume 1 or 2, shul-wide. A Shabbos is designated to launch the program and a siyum is scheduled for the end. Each shul also receives **'PRAYING WITH PASSION'** – a free (email) weekly newsletter with inspiring information and insights about a unique portion of the daily tefillah, as well as PDFs of flyers and posters encouraging participation, and a calendar with the learning dates for their community.

• **Project I.G.N.I.T.E – with NCSY/OU**

Impact: Over 1,000 NCSYers read Praying With Fire and many participated in national contest.

SCHOOL-WIDE TEFILLAH INITIATIVES

Elementary School Tefillah Initiative (Grades 5-8)

• To impart the concepts and underpinnings of tefillah at the child's level. This is available for grades 5-8. In the 2010-2011 school year, the test pilot project included over **1,500 students** in over **70 classes**.

- To provide children with a solid understanding and appreciation of the practical aspects of tefillah.

Emunah Through Tefillah Initiative

Impact: Strengthening Thousands of Students Around The World In Emunah

- This program helps students from high school grades and above build and strengthen their Emunah through Tefillah.

OTHER WORLDWIDE TEFILLAH INITIATIVES

- **Shliach Tzibbur Guide**

This guide provides a number of important Halachic points to guide the Shliach Tzibbur in properly discharging his duties.

- **Tefillin Awareness Project**

Thousands of men in almost 90 shuls in various communities benefited in properly fulfilling the mitzvah of tefillin.

- **VAT Tefillah Lecture Series**

'Praying With Fire' author travels to communities, shuls, and schools to inspire them about the importance and power of prayer, emunah and teshuvah.

For more information about these or any of our other initiatives, please contact us at **201.837.0354**, or fax to 201.837.7444, or e-mail info@prayingwithfire.org

The V'Ani Tefillah Foundation
1616 E. 29th St.
Brooklyn, NY 11229